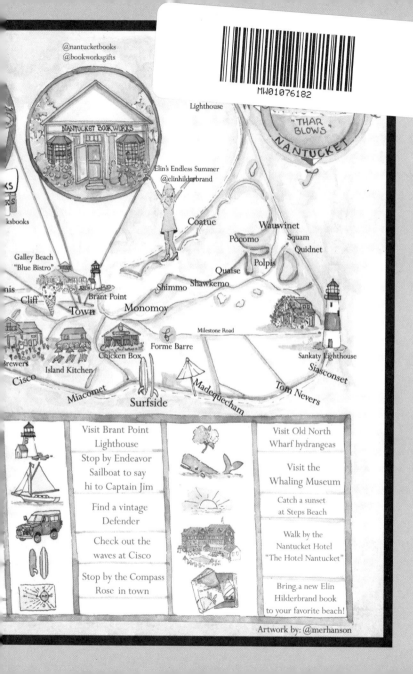

@nantucketbooks
@bookworksgifts

NANTUCKET BOOKWORKS

ksbooks

Lighthouse

"THAR BLOWS"
NANTUCKET

Elin's Endless Summer
@elinhilderbrand

Coatue

Wauwinet
Pocomo   Squam
                    Quidnet
Galley Beach
"Blue Bistro"   Polpis
                    Quaise
nis   Shawkemo
Cliff   Shimmo
        Brant Point
Town   Monomoy
                Milestone Road
        Forme Barre
                        Sankaty Lighthouse
Brewers   Siasconset
Island Kitchen
Cisco   Chicken Box
    Miacomet   Madequecham
        Surfside   Tom Nevers

	Visit Brant Point Lighthouse		Visit Old North Wharf hydrangeas
	Stop by Endeavor Sailboat to say hi to Captain Jim		Visit the Whaling Museum
	Find a vintage Defender		Catch a sunset at Steps Beach
	Check out the waves at Cisco		Walk by the Nantucket Hotel "The Hotel Nantucket"
	Stop by the Compass Rose in town		Bring a new Elin Hilderbrand book to your favorite beach!

Artwork by: @merhanson

The
Blue Book

ALSO BY ELIN HILDERBRAND

The
Blue Book

A MUST-SEE, CAN'T-MISS, WON'T-FORGET
• GUIDE TO NANTUCKET •

Elin Hilderbrand

With illustrations by Meredith Hanson

LITTLE, BROWN AND COMPANY
New York   Boston   London

Little, Brown and Company
Hachette Book Group
1290 Avenue of the Americas, New York, NY 10104
littlebrown.com

First Edition: May 2025

Little, Brown and Company is a division of Hachette Book Group, Inc. The Little, Brown name and logo are trademarks of Hachette Book Group, Inc.

The publisher is not responsible for websites (or their content) that are not owned by the publisher.

The Hachette Speakers Bureau provides a wide range of authors for speaking events. To find out more, go to hachettespeakersbureau.com or email hachettespeakers@hbgusa.com.

Little, Brown and Company books may be purchased in bulk for business, educational, or promotional use. For information, please contact your local bookseller or the Hachette Book Group Special Markets Department at special.markets@hbgusa.com.

Excerpt credits are on page 129.

Print book interior design by Taylor Navis

ISBN 9780316595834 (hc); 9780316597531 (signed edition)
LCCN 2024953014

10 9 8 7 6 5 4 3 2 1

FRI

Printed in Canada

This book is dedicated to Lizz and Elaine Backler,
the entire Bello family, Eileen Bratton, Jessica Jackson,
Mary Parker, and Marla Sofia: once readers, now cherished
friends...and honorary Nantucketers!

Contents

The
Blue Book

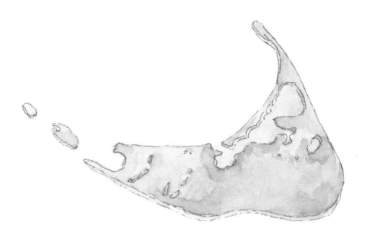

Introduction

In my novel *The Hotel Nantucket,* hotel manager Lizbet Keaton says, "The world needs a Nantucket guidebook written by an island insider." She offers guests of the (fictional) hotel a (fictional) recommendation guide called *The Blue Book.* Because I have, in real life, received messages and queries about where to go and what to do while on Nantucket, I decided to compile a list of my own recommendations.

The resulting *Blue Book* used to be available only as the end pages of *The Hotel Nantucket.*

Until now!

What I've learned in the past three years is that my readers have depended on *The Blue Book*! They've carted *The Hotel Nantucket* around, or they've copied the pages from the back. I thought to myself, *Wouldn't it be easier if we packaged* The Blue Book *as a stand-alone recommendation guide? And wouldn't it be fun to include scenes from my novels in which my characters are spending time in the locations mentioned?*

In taking another look at *The Blue Book,* I was also able to refresh information. (For example, I have a new favorite to add to my list of must-try Nantucket restaurants!) Although one of Nantucket's charms is that it stays pretty much the same, there are changes from year to year, and the guide you are now holding represents the most up-to-date information.

Please keep in mind that what follows is curated and very biased. It is not meant to be comprehensive. The places mentioned here are personal favorites, and *I have marked "can't-miss" locations with asterisks (**).* (I am not sponsored by any of the entities mentioned, nor given special treatment; I have as hard a time as anyone else getting a last-minute dinner reservation in the middle of August!) But *The Blue Book* will enhance any stay on the island—especially if you're an Elin Hilderbrand reader.

I hope you enjoy it. Welcome to Nantucket!

XOXO,
Elin

Two excellent resources for getting started on your trip planning are:

Nantucket Chamber of Commerce, 508-228-1700. Website: Nantucketchamber.org; Instagram: @ackchamber.

Town of Nantucket Culture & Tourism (known around town as Nantucket Visitor Services), 508-228-0925. Visitor Services keeps a list of available hotel rooms (and yes, there have been nights over the past few summers when the island was completely sold out!). Visitor Services offers all the practical information you'll need for your visit—and there are public restrooms adjacent to their office. Website: Nantucket-ma.gov.

Getting Here (and Back Home) Is the Hardest Part

ow much is the toll for the bridge?"

There is no bridge! Nantucket Island is thirty miles out to sea and therefore is accessible only by boat or plane. There are direct flights from New York (JFK), Newark, Washington, DC, and certain other cities in the summer on JetBlue, United, American, and Delta. Cape Air runs a nine-seat Cessna from Boston and JFK year-round. (Warning: These Cessnas are not for the faint of heart. I will not include the scene from *Golden Girl* that takes place on a Cape Air flight because I don't want to scare anyone. Although these flights can be bumpy, they are perfectly safe.)

We also have ferries, known on the island as the "fast boat" and the "slow boat." The slow boat is operated by the Steamship Authority and is the only way to bring a vehicle. If you want to bring your car or truck to Nantucket, you must get a reservation (and these sell out *way* in advance, starting in January!). You are of course welcome to come with your own bikes on the ferry for a nominal fee.

My preferred mode of travel to and from the island is the fast ferry. From April through December, both the Steamship Authority and Hy-Line Cruises operate ferries throughout the day—and the Hy-Line runs ferry service year-round. The trip takes an hour; round trip costs less than $90. Pro tip: The Hy-Line offers special seating called Captain's View for $10 more per ticket in the summer but only $3 more per ticket in the off-season. This seating comes with priority boarding and is very comfortable; it's located on the second level, in the bow of the boat.

Weather often affects travel to and from the island. If the wind is blowing twenty-five miles per hour or faster, the ferries may cancel (each trip is at the discretion of the captain). If there is fog (which there often is in June and early July), planes are grounded. (Fun fact: Tom Nevers Field was used by the US military in World War II to practice taking off and landing in the fog.) Being stranded either on Nantucket or trying to get to Nantucket is considered part of life for Nantucketers, so make sure your plans are flexible.

Once on Nantucket, you can either rent a Jeep (**Nantucket Windmill Auto Rental, Nantucket Island Rent-A-Car**) or rent a bike (**Young's Bicycle Shop, Nantucket Bike Shop, Cook's Cycles,** or **Easy Riders Bicycle Rentals,** which will deliver bikes to your lodging!). The island also has Uber, Lyft, and a host of taxis. My favorite taxi company is **Roger's Taxi,** 508-818-8294. **Cranberry Transportation** provides a proper "car service," and they also give private tours of the island.

Where Should I Stay?

I wrote an entire novel called *The Hotel Nantucket,* so I'll start by recommending the inspiration for the "main character" in that book, which is the **Nantucket Hotel****, located at 77 Easton Street. Although the hotel in the book is a creation of my imagination, the real Nantucket Hotel does have certain similarities: It has both rooms and suites, a family pool and an adult pool, a fabulous fitness center, a yoga studio, and a newly renovated bar/restaurant. The staff is professional and friendly, and like the hotel in the book, the real hotel is located on the edge of town, within easy walking distance of not only shopping, restaurants, museums, and galleries but also **Children's Beach, Jetties Beach,** and **Brant Point Lighthouse.** Even if you aren't staying at the Nantucket, you should drop by for a visit—or for lunch at **Sailor's Valentine,** on the hotel's outdoor porch. Then you can say you visited "the Hotel Nantucket." Website: Thenantuckethotel.com; Instagram: @thenantucket.

The only accommodation that is directly *on* the beach is **Cliffside Beach Club,** which was the inspiration for my first novel, *The Beach Club.* Cliffside's lobby is one of the most spectacular spaces on the island. The hotel has twenty-three rooms (where you step out *into sand*), a pool and a fitness center, a small private café, and a private beach on Nantucket Sound. (The water is calm, and good for swimming.) Cliffside is a splurge—if you can get in! Website: Cliffsidebeach.com; Instagram: @cliffsidebeachclub.

76 Main Ink Press Hotel offers the ultimate experience for Elin Hilderbrand fans, as they have an "Elin" suite. This suite is beachy and fun, with photos of me and my book covers, and there's a director's chair from the set of *The Perfect Couple,* the adaptation of my novel. I even signed a beam in the room! The hotel is right smack in the middle of town, so everything you may need is a short walk away. The suite opens onto 76 Main's adorable courtyard. Website: 76main.com; Instagram: @76main.

Greydon House used to be a private home and dentist's office, but it has been lavishly remodeled into a cozy boutique hotel with an unbelievably good restaurant, **Via Mare.** I have stayed at Greydon House twice myself on staycations, and I loved the delicious breakfasts, the custom-tiled showers, and the ideal in-town location. Website: Greydonhouse.com; Instagram: @greydonhouse.

When you *really* want to get away from it all, check out the **Wauwinet** inn. It's nine miles out of town (this is *very* far by Nantucket standards), but the drive takes you along the beautiful, winding Polpis Road, where you'll pass farms, ponds, and the **Nantucket Shipwreck & Lifesaving Museum.** The Wauwinet is located on the harbor at the entry to **Great Point.** The hotel has an expansive deck lined with Adirondack chairs that overlook the harbor. There's a library, a charming tucked-away bar, and a fine-dining restaurant, **Topper's,** which is where Benji takes Celeste in my novel *The Perfect Couple.* Website: Wauwinet.com; Instagram: @thewauwinet.

from *The Perfect Couple*

Dinner at Topper's is an extraordinary experience, with attention given to every detail. Drinks are brought on a tiered cocktail tray; Benji's gin and tonic is mixed at the table with a glass swizzle stick. The bread basket features warm, fragrant rosemary focaccia, homemade bacon-and-sage rolls, and twisted cheddar-garlic breadsticks that look like the branches of a tree in an enchanted forest. Under other circumstances, Celeste would be committing all this to memory so she could describe it for her parents later, but she is preoccupied with the one sentence written on the note that was slipped under her door. *In case you have any doubts, I'm in love with you.*

Their appetizers arrive under silver domes. The server lifts both domes at once with a theatrical flourish. The food is artwork—vegetables are cut to resemble jewels; sauces are painted across plates. Benji ordered a wine that is apparently so rare and amazing it made the sommelier stammer.

I Have a Place to Stay and a Way to Get Around. Now What Do I Do?

You're on an island, so let's start at the beach! Nantucket has fifty miles of coastline, most of it open to the public. Some of it has auto access, but you'll need a four-wheel-drive vehicle with the proper sticker. For beaches such as **40th Pole** and **Smith's Point,** you'll need a town beach sticker, yours for $100. (You can procure one of these at the police station—and hey, maybe you'll see Chief Kapenash!) The sticker to access Great Point is purchased at the entry; it costs $160 (you can also get a day pass for $60). Most rental vehicles available on Nantucket come with these stickers. *Before you drive onto the beach,* you must let the air in your tires down to fifteen pounds (you can go lower for Great Point; there are two air hoses to refill when you're heading back to civilization, just past the guardhouse). Trust me: The last thing you want to do is get "stuck" on the beach like Kacy and Coco in my novel *Swan Song.*

from *Swan Song*

"Let me move the Jeep," Kacy says, "so that it blocks the wind."

Coco has her eyes closed and doesn't answer.

Kacy climbs in the Jeep and throws it into reverse, but it won't budge. She senses she's about to face a reckoning. She hits the gas a little harder; the tires spin, chewing deeper into the sand. She shifts the car into drive, though she has to be careful because the front of the Jeep is dangerously close to the water. Was she really that careless, or has the tide come in? *Both,* she thinks. The Jeep edges forward a few inches and Kacy is heartened. She moves up a bit more, thinking, *Forget the wind block, I just need to get the Jeep on firmer ground.* But she succeeds only in putting her front two tires into wet sand, which is very bad. She tries to back up — nope. She turns the wheel, but this takes her closer to the water.

No! she thinks.

Here are my thoughts on drive-on beaches: I love them. This love intensified when I had children. Instead of schlepping all of our stuff from whatever parking spot I happened to find (if I found a parking spot—because when you have kids it's challenging to get out of the house in a timely fashion), I just pulled onto the beach, and all of their stuff was right there in the back of the car. There were years when the kids napped in the car, windows wide open. There were years when the kids climbed on the car (I had Jeeps; they were rugged vehicles). There were years when my kids climbed on my friends' cars (even better). Because you can drive on, 40th Pole is particularly good for evening beach barbecues with kids: the water is calm and warm, and you'll have a magnificent view of the sunset.

Smith's Point, which is open only during certain weeks of the summer, depending on the nesting of the endangered piping plover, is hands down my favorite beach because you can access both the waves of the ocean and the flat water of the sound. There's also a natural water slide as described in my novel *The Perfect Couple*.

from *The Perfect Couple*

Celeste and Shooter drive up over the dunes. The stark natural beauty of Smith's Point is staggering. There's a long stretch of pristine beach in front of them, with the ocean to the left and dunes carpeted in eelgrass to the right. Beyond those dunes is the flat blue surface of Nantucket Sound.

Shooter is taking it slow—five miles an hour—so he can easily reach over to the glove compartment, grazing Celeste's knee with the back of his hand as he does so. He pulls out a guide to eastern shorebirds.

Right away, Celeste points out the sandpiper and the American oystercatcher with its signature orange beak. Shooter laughs and says, "You delight me." He drives out to the tip of Smith's

Point—Celeste sees the much smaller island of Tuckernuck across a narrow channel—and then he curves around to the far side of the point. He sets up a camp—a chair for each of them, an umbrella for shade, towels, and a small table, where he lays out their lunch. He shucks off his polo shirt. Celeste tries not to notice the muscles of his back.

"Watch this," he says. He wades out into the water a few feet and then he must drop off a ledge or a shelf because suddenly he is in up to his chest. He lifts his hands in the air, and the water whooshes him down the shore. "Yeehaw!" he cries out. About forty yards down, he climbs out of the water and jogs back to Celeste. "It's a natural water slide," he says. "You have to try it."

Great Point is Nantucket's ultimate destination. **Great Point Light** sits at the tippy top of the long arm of sand that juts into the water to the north. Great Point is a nature preserve, hence the hefty sticker price. It's a wild, windswept landscape—with ocean on your right and the harbor on your left as you drive out. There are almost always seals. There are sometimes sharks—you've been warned! It *is* "far away" (it takes nearly forty-five minutes to get there from town), but it's a Nantucket experience you'll never forget.

Some people think driving on a beach is an abomination. I respect that—and so does Nantucket. Most beaches do not allow cars. Here are some of my favorites that you CANNOT drive on. North shore beaches front Nantucket Sound and have calm water without large waves. South shore beaches are ocean beaches and normally have waves. There are sometimes rip currents. Please be careful!

NORTH SHORE

Jetties Beach is walkable from town and has the added attraction of **Sandbar,** which I'll discuss in the restaurant chapter. **Steps Beach** has, quite possibly, the most beautiful approach of any beach in the world. You descend a long flight of steps down into sand dunes covered by rosa rugosa, which in the height of summer blooms with pink and white flowers. **Dionis Beach** offers public restrooms, which made it a favorite of Richie's in *The Hotel Nantucket.*

from *The Hotel Nantucket*

Officer Dixon gets a call at four o'clock in the afternoon about a man asleep in his car at Dionis Beach.

"So what?" Dixon says to Sheila in dispatch.

"I guess he's been sleeping in his car in the parking lot the past three days," Sheila says. "Some mommy noticed him and thinks he's a potential predator."

Dixon takes a breath. A man sleeping in his car is what passes for crime on Nantucket; he supposes he should be glad. He climbs into his cruiser.

When he arrives at Dionis, he sees the man and the car in question—some guy in his early fifties in a 2010 Honda Pilot with Connecticut plates and a WHAT WOULD JIM CALHOUN DO? bumper sticker. The back window sports a decal that says PARENT OF AN AVON MIDDLE SCHOOL HONOR STUDENT.

Threatening stuff. Dixon wonders if he'll need to call for backup. He approaches the open car window and sees the guy in the driver's seat, head slumped back, snoring away. He's wearing a white polo shirt and swim trunks; his bifocals have slid down to the end of his nose, and there's a copy of Lee Child's *Blue Moon* splayed open in the console next to an open Red Bull. Dixon backs away because he feels like he's intruding on the guy in his bedroom—and then he notices the open shaving kit on the passenger seat and a hand towel drying on the dashboard. A peek into the back seat reveals a gaping suitcase.

Is this guy…Dixon glances over at the public bathrooms. Dionis is the only beach on Nantucket that has showers. Is this guy *living* in his car?

"Excuse me, sir," Dixon says, jostling the guy's shoulder. "May I see your license and registration, please?"

SOUTH SHORE

Surfside Beach was my beach of choice for my first three summers on the island. In fact, I don't think I went anywhere else. It's *wide.* There's plenty of *space.* It also has the beach shack restaurant the **Surf****. It's not an exaggeration to say that if I could, I would eat lunch at the Surf every day of the summer, and so would my kids. The food is *delicious.* I get the Crabby Patty (crab, shrimp, and scallop patty) with avocado, bacon, lettuce, tomato, and their delicious sauce. My daughter gets the acai bowl. The boys get the grilled chicken sandwich or burgers. It falls into my "can't-miss" category if you're staying on Nantucket for more than one day during the summer. However, there is often a line—you've been warned!

Nobadeer Beach: Are you twenty-five or younger? Go here. It's party central. There's a walk-on section and a drive-on section. Both are filled with beautiful young people living their best lives. If you're walking on, be sure to park in the lot and not on the road—you will get a ticket.

Cisco: Do you surf or like to watch other people surf? Go here, where you can also take lessons at **Nantucket Island Surf School** (website: Nantucketsurfing.com), run by island surf legend Gary Kohner. For those of you who aren't surfing, be aware that the beach is much narrower than at Surfside and Nobadeer, and parking is often an issue.

None of these is my favorite beach. I have thought long and hard and decided not to name my preferred south shore beach because what I love about it is that it's not popular and is never very crowded, except with locals and summer residents. Because I feel guilty for gatekeeping, I will say that if you want a terrific not-crowded beach, drive out to **Miacomet Golf Course,** but just before you reach the clubhouse, take a right onto the dirt road that leads past the big antenna. The road is what I have called in my books "the no-name road," and the beach is what I call Antenna Beach. A cottage to the left of the entrance to this beach was the inspiration for Mallory's cottage in *28 Summers.*

from *28 Summers*

On the beach, Mallory calls Frazier's name and Jake jogs along the waterline. The waves slam the shore with uncharacteristic force, or maybe it just seems that way because it's so late and so dark.

There are some stars, but clouds cover the moon, and there are no other homes on this stretch of beach, no homes until Cisco, nearly a mile away. Mallory has never realized how isolated her cottage is.

What Is There to Do If I Don't Like the Beach?

Yes, I do realize there are people who don't like the beach. (I am grateful that you like beach novels!)

DO YOU LIKE TO SHOP?

If the answer is yes, you're in luck! Unlike Martha's Vineyard, which has seven towns, Nantucket has only one town, called "town." (Locals say, "I'm going to town." Or "I saw Elin in town.") Nantucket's central business district is four square blocks, filled with unique shopping (remember: no chain stores), all of it adjacent to the ferry docks. It's therefore possible to get off the ferry, shop, get something to eat, and get back on the ferry—and although you will not have seen nearly enough of the island, you also won't be disappointed. Town is just that great.

There are too many shops for me to mention, so I'm giving you only my very favorites.

Mitchell's Book Corner and **Nantucket Bookworks****: Hmm…why did I start with these? Well, because I believe independent bookstores are the cornerstones of civilization. Nantucket is lucky enough to have not one but two independents, and they're owned by the same person, my cherished friend Wendy Hudson. The good news about Wendy owning both stores is that instead of being competitors, they complement each other. Mitchell's is located at 54 Main Street and has two floors of books, including an outstanding selection of Nantucket-based books. From early June to early October, I do a book signing upstairs at Mitchell's every Wednesday at 11 a.m. for the first 120 people who get in line. (This signing ends promptly at noon, when the church bells ring.) Mitchell's hosts signings all year round, including frequent signings with my fellow local authors Nancy Thayer and Nathaniel Philbrick. Website: Nantucketbookpartners.com; Instagram: @nantucketbooks.

Nantucket Bookworks can be found at 25 Broad Street. It's quaint and cozy and has an outstanding children's books section; a huge selection of toys, games, and gifts; and chocolate!

The biggest celebrity at these bookstores is the events and marketing director, Tim Ehrenberg, who has a Bookstagram account, @timtalksbooks, where he gives outstanding recommendations. If Tim tells me to read it, I read it, and you should too!

Flowers on Chestnut**: If there's one store other than the bookstores that I would say you can't miss, it's Flowers on Chestnut. Most visitors aren't in need of a florist, but you should stop into Flowers anyway just for the aesthetics. There's a sumptuous floral display in the middle of the first floor and a charming side garden. Flowers also has a divine selection of candles, gifts, antiques, greeting cards, wrapping paper, cocktail napkins, and home furnishings. Website: Flowersonchestnut.com; Instagram: @flowersonchestnut.

Jessica Hicks Jewelry**: I bought my first pair of Jessica Hicks earrings in 2008, and now, over fifteen years later, I have well over a hundred pieces, including the silver thumb ring featured in *The Perfect Couple,* 5 Star Earrings in silver, and a *Swan Song* necklace. Jessica's shop is tucked just off Main on Union Street—it's a must-visit for any Elin Hilderbrand reader. Her pieces have a wide range of prices, with something for every budget. Website: Jessicahicks.com; Instagram: @jessicahicksjewelry.

from *The Perfect Couple*

Tag…has been trained by Greer to understand that the only acceptable present for a birthday or anniversary is jewelry. He walks into the Jessica Hicks boutique thinking he will get earrings or a choker, but when he describes the young woman he's buying for—he pretends the gift is for his daughter-in-law, Abby, who is pregnant with their first grandchild—Jessica shows him the silver ring with the lace pattern embedded with the multicolored sapphires.

"It's meant to be worn on the thumb," Jessica says.

"The thumb?" Tag says.

"Trust me," Jessica says. "It's a thing."

Tag buys the thumb ring and leaves the store feeling a sense of giddy anticipation. The ring is beautiful; Merritt will love it, he's certain.

His happiness is a thing.

The Hub of Nantucket: As the name suggests (just call it the Hub), this newsstand (which also has books, magazines, candy, souvenirs, gifts, coffee, and smoothies) is in the middle of town, on the corner of Main Street and Federal. Website: Thehubofnantucket.com; Instagram: @thehubofnantucket.

Nantucket Looms**: Oh, how I love Looms. The hydrangea-blue cashmere blanket in *The Hotel Nantucket* started out as a figment of my imagination…until Nantucket Looms created one, available on a limited basis. (They gifted me this blanket and it is so soft and luxurious, I won't let any of my children near it!) Looms has an impressive selection of woven goods as well as furniture and art. They also sell two kinds of wildflower soap, which is my go-to hostess gift. Website: Nantucketlooms .com; Instagram: @nantucketlooms.

Blue Beetle**: My favorite place for cashmere: ponchos, wraps, and sweaters, especially Nantucket sweaters. Possibly my favorite purchase of the past decade was the heather gray sweater with a rainbow-striped ACK on the front. (ACK is the airport designation for Nantucket.) They also have sweaters with the island on the front (I have this in four colors!). Website: Bluebeetlenantucket .com; Instagram: @bluebeetlenantucket.

Erica Wilson: Erica Wilson was a pioneer in the world of needlepoint. This shop on Main Street is still partially dedicated to the art (you can buy canvases of Elin book covers here!) — and the other half is women's fashion. I nearly always find something wonderful. The shop features the jewelry of **Heidi Weddendorf** (Instagram: @heidiweddendorf), which I often wear when I'm out on a book tour. Website: Ericawilson.com; Instagram: @ericawilsonnantucket.

Milly & Grace**: Perhaps my favorite women's clothing boutique on the island, this shop, named for owner Emily Ott's grandmothers, also has home goods. This is where I first found the round towels by the Beach People and bought my very first S'well bottle. Website: Millyand grace.com; Instagram: @shopmillyandgrace.

Hepburn Nantucket: Another must when you're looking for women's fashion. Many of the dresses you see me wearing on Instagram came from Hepburn, and this was where I bought my very first pair of Mystique sandals! Website: Hepburnnantucket.com; Instagram: @hepburnnantucket.

Centre Pointe**: Located at 22 Centre Street, this boutique is filled with unique, tasteful home goods as well as fashion. Owner Margaret Anne Nolen founded her own line called Cartolina (Italian for "postcard"). I wore Cartolina's Hadley romper in my 2024 shoot for the *Wall Street Journal,* and my characters also wear Cartolina — including Lizbet in *The Hotel Nantucket* and Blond Sharon in *Swan Song.* Website: 28centrepointe.com; Instagram: @centrepointenantucket.

Murray's Toggery Shop**: Murray's is…the OG of Nantucket's shopping scene. It is…the home of prep. It is…the home of, wait for it, Nantucket Reds, the infamous "red" fabric that starts out a certain shade of brick and becomes, with each washing, more and more faded until it reaches its goal: a unique and unmistakable pale pink. The Murray family invented not only this color, but also, in a sense, a philosophical principle held dear on Nantucket: the older and more battered an article of clothing (or a Jeep Wrangler or a lightship basket), the more authentic. To wear a brand-new pair of Nantucket Reds to dinner is considered gauche. Wash them thirty times first, then don them at every opportunity—when you're surf casting at Smith's Point, when you're selecting tomatoes at **Bartlett's Ocean View Farm,** when you're dancing in the front row at the **Chicken Box.** Spill your gin and tonic on them. Stand in the sea spray of the ferry. That's what they're made for. Nantucket Reds come in pants, skirts, children's overalls, and other assorted styles and *can only be properly purchased* at Murray's Toggery Shop. (Note: Murray's also has other clothing. I spent many a panicked two-days-before-prom at Murray's with both of my boys, trying on pants, shirts, ties, and jackets.) It's a family-owned-and-run business that has a magical, old-school feel. Don't miss it. Website: Nantucket reds.com; Instagram: @ackreds.

Barnaby's Toy & Art Shack**: Are you looking for a fun place to take your young kids? Beloved children's book character Barnaby Bear's world expanded when author and illustrator Wendy Rouillard opened Barnaby's Toy & Art Shack. Barnaby's is a whole experience—a curated toy store that offers art classes such as beading, fairy house building, and wood slice art, as well as a drop-in art studio where children can create any time of day. If you have little people, Barnaby's is a must. Also available for birthday parties and private events (once, when I walked in, a dude was teaching the kids magic!). They also sell great neon-lit outlines of Nantucket Island (I have one!). Website: Barnabystoyandart.com; Instagram @barnabybearbooks.

Force Five and Broad Street Surf Shop: If your children are a bit older—ten to seventeen, say—chances are they will want to make a stop at the surf shop and clothier Force Five. Force Five has the added attraction of a hidden candy room in the back of the store. Broad Street Surf Shop, on the Strip, is smaller but has everything to fulfill your dreams of becoming the next Alana Blanchard. Instagrams: @force5nantucket and @broadstreetsurf.

ARE YOU IN THE MARKET FOR ART OR PHOTOGRAPHY?

Town is filled with galleries. The two I am fondest of are Coe & Co on Main Street—Nathan Coe's art photography is chic and sexy—and the Samuel Owen Gallery, where I bought my "slushie wave" by photographer Jonathan Nimerfroh (Instagram: @jdnphotography). Websites: Coeandcogallery.com and Samuelowen.com; Instagrams: @candcphotographygallery and @samuelowen.

If you want to take home a piece of Nantucket, you should

check out the surf landscapes by **Lauren Marttila** (website: Laurenmarttilaphotography.com; Instagram: @lauren marttilaphotography). I have these photographs throughout my house. Another island artist whose work I both collect and write about is the landscape painter **Illya Kagan** (website: Illyakagan.com; Instagram: @illyakagan).

ARE YOU A HISTORY BUFF?

Perhaps the most robust nonprofit on Nantucket is the **Nantucket Historical Association.** The NHA's most popular site is the **Nantucket Whaling Museum** on Broad Street, but the NHA also owns and operates the **Hadwen House**

at the top of Main Street (across from the famous **Three Bricks**), the **Old Mill,** the **Oldest House,** and perhaps my favorite of the NHA properties, **Greater Light.** Built as a livestock barn in 1790, Greater Light was purchased and reimagined as an artist's oasis by two unmarried Quaker sisters, Gertrude and Hannah Monaghan. Greater Light has been lovingly restored, including the exquisite gardens, to its former glory by the NHA. To get updates on tour dates and times, visit Nha.org; Instagram: @ackhistory.

The **Nantucket Preservation Trust** operates walking tours of downtown Nantucket during the summer months. Website: Nantucketpreservation.org.

One great way to see "all" of Nantucket at once is to visit the **First Congregational Church** and climb up to the tower. The tower has panoramic views across the island; it's Nantucket's answer to the Empire State Building—and it's where my runaway bride ends up in *Beautiful Day.*

from *Beautiful Day*

Beth had asked for her ashes to be scattered from the Congregational Church tower because it looked out over the whole island. Doug, fearing that tossing his wife's remains from the tower window might be frowned upon by the church staff, or possibly even deemed illegal, had suggested they smuggle Beth's ashes up the stairs. They had gone at the very end of the day, after all the other tourists had vacated, and the surreptitious nature of their mission had made it feel mischievous, even fun—and the somberness of the occasion had been alleviated a bit. Margot had stuffed the box of ashes in her Fendi hobo bag, and Kevin had pried open a window at the top. Beth's remains had fallen softly, like snowflakes. Most of her ashes had landed on the church's green lawn, but Margot imagined that bits had been carried farther afield

by the breeze. She lay in the treetops, on the gambrel roofs; she dusted the streets and fertilized the pocket gardens.

ARE YOU A MOVIE BUFF?

There is only one official movie theater on Nantucket, and it's a beauty. The **Dreamland Theater** underwent a gut renovation in 2012 and is now, in my humble opinion, one of the most stunning (and energy-efficient) movie theaters in America. Open year-round! I served as chairperson for the Dream Believer benefit in 2020, which was the year the **Dreamland Drive-In** movie theater was started (the drive-in operates only in the summer), and I was incredibly honored to receive the DreamBIG award in the summer of 2024. This theater is also where we held the premiere of the Netflix series *The Perfect Couple.* Website: Nantucket dreamland.org; Instagram: @nantucketdreamland.

What Is "Sconset" Anyway?

S conset" is short for Siasconset (no one calls it Siasconset), which is the village on the eastern end of
the island. Sconset has its own vibe (and the residents will no doubt bristle at my use of the word "vibe").
Sconset is understated; it's old-school and it despises

pretension. Life in Sconset is slower; bumper stickers read TWENTY IS PLENTY IN SCONSET. (This refers to the speed limit.) In Sconset you're likely to see children on tricycles pedaling down the street and people in straw hats pruning roses; you'll see picket fences and 1988 Jeep Wagoneers with a rainbow stripe of beach stickers across the back bumper. It's easy to be a tourist in Sconset but nearly impossible to become a bona fide "Sconseter"—unless you were lucky enough to buy property there during the Ford administration.

Two roads lead to Sconset. One is the Milestone Road, which is the only state-maintained road on Nantucket. It's seven miles long, relatively straight and flat, and fairly uneventful except for the stone markers at every mile (and at pi, 3.14 miles from town). As you get out toward mile marker five, you'll have a nice vista so reminiscent of the African savannah that certain artistic pranksters cut and painted life-size elephants and lions that make appearances from time to time; look out for them as you drive or bicycle past.

The other way to get to Sconset is via the long and winding Polpis Road. Polpis takes you past stone walls and wooden fences, a dramatic overwater view at the Nantucket Shipwreck & Lifesaving Museum, and the turnoffs for the Wauwinet and **Quidnet,** and then past **Sesachacha Pond,** where you'll glimpse **Sankaty Head Light** in the distance before cruising past **Sankaty Head Golf Club.** The Polpis Road is nine miles long. Both Polpis and Milestone have bike paths, and the very fit and enthusiastic choose to do the "loop." You can also bike out to Sconset one way and then put your bike on the front of the **Wave,** Nantucket's public transportation, and get a ride home!

I MADE IT TO SCONSET. NOW WHAT DO I DO?

Sconset is famous for its colony of summer cottages, many of them tiny, many of them old (some of the oldest houses on the island are in Sconset, including a house called **Auld Lang Syne:** part of it was constructed around 1675!), and many of them, at the end of June and beginning of July, draped in cottage roses. There is no experience on Nantucket that is more storybook than wandering the quiet streets of Sconset when the roses are in bloom. I go every year—and every year, I am left breathless.

Along Baxter Road is the **Sconset Bluff Walk,** a path on the cliff above the Atlantic. You can walk out Baxter Road all the way to Sankaty Head Light, which looks like a peppermint stick.

You can also meander down Ocean Ave to the **Summer House,** a hotel with a pool that fronts the ocean. There's a footbridge where you'll see a large sundial on the side of a private home. The bridge will lead you to the Sconset Rotary, where you'll find **Claudette's** sandwich shop (outstanding turkey salad), a package store, a tiny post office with irregular hours, the **Sconset Café** (home of the chocolate volcano cake), and finally the **Sconset Market****. The market is the beating heart of town—it has not only groceries but ice-cream cones, and not only ice-cream cones but freshly baked baguettes every day!

Along New Street in Sconset are the **Siasconset Casino,** the **Siasconset Union Chapel,** and the **Chanticleer.** This little stretch shouldn't be missed. The Sconset Casino is now a tennis club, but it's also an event space used for weddings and benefits, and it occasionally hosts movies in the summer. It was once used as a summer stage for the Broadway actors of the 1920s who chose to vacation on Nantucket. It's a building that evokes the era of old Nantucket.

The Siasconset Union Chapel is an ecumenical chapel used for services in the summer. (I was once married in this church!) The Sconset Chapel evokes a peaceful simplicity, and all of the kneelers were needlepointed by parishioners. One unusual feature is the columbarium in the memorial gardens, where the ashes of Sconset residents (and *only* Sconset residents) are tucked into a tasteful wall.

The Chanticleer will be mentioned in the restaurant chapter, but even if you're not planning on eating there, you should be sure to snap a picture of the front garden with its iconic carousel horse.

I set my novel *Barefoot* out in Sconset; Vicki, Brenda, Melanie, and the kids live in one of the tiny cottages on Shell Street.

from *Barefoot*

The cabbie said, "Where to?" And Brenda said, "Shell Street, Sconset."

The cottage had been built in 1803 — back, Vicki thought, when life was both busier and simpler, back when people were shorter and held lower expectations. The cottage had originally been one room with a fireplace built into the north wall, but over the years, three "warts" had been added for bedrooms. All of the rooms were small with low ceilings; it was like living in a dollhouse. That was what Aunt Liv had loved about the cottage — it was life pared down, scaled way back. There was no TV, no answering machine, no computer or microwave or stereo. It was a true summerhouse, Aunt Liv used to say, because it encouraged you to spend most of your time outside — on the back deck overlooking the yard and garden, or down the street at Sconset's public beach.

In a Category by Itself: Cisco Brewers**

D ubbed by *Men's Health* magazine "the happiest place on earth," **Cisco Brewers** is, in modern parlance, a "whole thing." There are three barns—one housing a beer bar, one a wine bar, and one a spirits bar—serving Cisco products, including their popular Whale's Tale Pale Ale, Gripah, Triple Eight vodka, and my go-to, the sparkling cranberry pinot gris. However—and I do not say this lightly—alcohol is the least important thing about the place. This is a center of joy. There are food trucks: **167Raw** for raw bar and guacamole, **Nantucket Poke** for bowls and tartare, and the **Nantucket Lobster Trap** for swordfish sliders and lobster rolls. There is often live music. There are dogs and children and people relaxing at open-air picnic tables alongside the gardens that provide the produce and herbs for the mixed drinks. It is the *ultimate* après-beach scene, a must for any Sunday fun day, and just generally a destination you should not miss. For teetotalers, there are handcrafted sodas as well. Cisco has proved so popular that satellite locations have popped up in places like the Boston Seaport; Portsmouth, New Hampshire; and Stamford, Connecticut. Website: Ciscobrewers.com; Instagram: @ciscobrewers.

I have mentioned Cisco Brewers and its products in several books, and it's where Harper and Ramsay go for lunch in *The Identicals.*

from *The Identicals*

It's the lunch hour, and places will be crowded, Ramsay says, so he suggests "the brewery" because Harper can bring her dog.

Brilliant, Harper thinks. *Ramsay is thoughtful.* And, as it turns out, the brewery—CISCO BREWERS, the sign says—is the perfect laid-back place to go on a mild, sunny afternoon.

Harper loves Nantucket already!

The brewery features a large brick patio surrounded by rustic farm buildings. One building sells beer, another sells wine, and yet another sells spirits. Perched on a stool with a golden retriever at his feet is a long-haired guy playing the guitar. There are a few dozen people sitting at picnic tables, drinking and eating guacamole and chips or oysters from the food trucks. Ramsay and Harper choose an empty picnic table, and Ramsay says, "How does a beer and a lobster roll sound?"

Harper loves a man who instinctively knows what a particular moment calls for. "Like heaven," she says.

To Market, to Market . . .

If you're in search of a regular grocery store, the island has two **Stop & Shops**. There's one downtown on the harbor, but this store is smaller than the newly renovated mid-island branch, which has the advantage of an attached family-run package store: **Nantucket Wine & Spirits.** Website: Nantucketwineandspirits.com; Instagram: @nantucketwines.

Bartlett's Ocean View Farm** has appeared in nearly every single one of my novels. The farm itself is 160 acres of fields including photogenic rows of flowers, like something out of a Renoir painting. It also has a nursery for all of your gardening and landscaping needs, as well as a fabulous market. I go to the farm two or three times a week in the summer. Here are the things I love about Bartlett's: a selection of fresh flowers, including the lilies that grace my kitchen all summer long; homemade pies (I choose peach and blueberry); and the prepared foods (this is where I source my lobster salad, and I also love their broccoli slaw). Produce! In mid-July the corncrib appears, and then come the tomatoes (although Bartlett's also has outstanding hothouse tomatoes). I also adore their organic lettuces, which come washed in bags. In fall: pumpkins and gourds. Website: Bartletts farm.com; Instagram: @bartlettsfarm.

The farm is also where Hollis buys provisions for her five-star weekend!

from *The Five-Star Weekend*

Long before Molly Beardsley is awake in California, Hollis is driving past a field of lilies, zinnias, cosmos, and snapdragons in rainbow-hued rows at Bartlett's Farm. It's a vista worthy of Monet, of Renoir, and Hollis considers stopping to take a picture, but she's on a mission. She pulls into the parking lot of the farm market at 7:55.

She did end up reading some of the debate on her website. Is it too soon for Hollis to be hosting a girls' weekend?

Oh, probably, she thinks. But it has lifted her spirits and given her something to look forward to. And since she's throwing it, she'll do it her way. End of discussion.

At eight o'clock sharp, market manager Lily Callahan (who happens to be a frequent visitor to the Hungry with Hollis website; she knows what Hollis is doing here!) flips the sign to OPEN.

Just inside the front door, Hollis stops at the display of fresh flowers. There are galvanized-metal buckets of lilies in white, yellow, peach, and something called "double pink." Hollis selects five stems, then chooses four mixed bouquets that were picked earlier that morning, their petals still damp from the sprinklers. Then it's on to the corn. The ears are snugged into the crib side by side and end to end like a neat puzzle. (Lily Callahan loves to look at the corncrib first thing in the morning. By late afternoon, the corn will be ravaged by people stopping by after the beach, ears flung willy-nilly and half stripped despite the sign that says PLEASE DO NOT SHUCK THE CORN!) Next, Hollis selects hothouse tomatoes, organic butter lettuce, cucumbers, zucchini, and summer squash. She moves on to the herbs: fresh dill, fresh basil, a bunch of chives, and what Lily and the rest of the staff refer to as "porn-star mint" (it's very well-endowed). Hollis glides her cart over to the cheese case, where she chooses Taleggio and a clothbound cheddar (five-star cheese; Lily approves!), fancy crackers, a couple sticks of Italian salami, Marcona almonds, a can of salt-and-pepper Virginia peanuts (they're ridiculously addictive), and Alfonso olives.

Moors End Farm: Set along the Polpis Road, some islanders insist that Moors End Farm has even better corn than Bartlett's. (Quarrels have broken out on the topic.) And at the holidays, this is where EVERYONE, including yours truly, sources their Christmas trees, wreaths, and garlands. Website: Moorsendfarm.com; Instagram: @moorsendfarm.

Pip and Anchor is one of Nantucket's newest markets and it's on an "eat local" mission. Everything sold at Pip is grown or produced within a hundred miles of the island. The produce is unparalleled, and they have an extensive wine offering. They also sell cheese, condiments, crackers and chips, meat and seafood, dairy and eggs. They run a brisk coffee business as well as serving made-to-order sandwiches. This thoughtful, intentional place should not be missed! Website: Pipandanchor.com; Instagram: @pipandanchor.

from *Swan Song*

Down the street at Pip and Anchor, [Coco] buys Leslee's usual organic rosé and her Savage cheese, then goes on a spree in the jams and spreads section. She throws a bottle of homemade ketchup into her basket along with cider syrup and a jar of strawberry Italian plum rosewater jam (for the name alone). Leslee has never once asked Coco for a receipt, never questioned a charge, so why not indulge?

Nantucket Meat & Fish Market is a favorite of mine. For starters, the meat and fish case is something to behold. Forgive me, vegans: I get the house-marinated steak tips and the gorgeous burgers with cheese and bacon already incorporated (I have hungry children at home!). The market features a host of gourmet groceries, sushi, and the only Starbucks concession on the island; it's where my daughter gets her "pink drink." Website: Nantucketmeat andfish.com; Instagram: @ack_meatandfish.

I first wrote about Nantucket Meat & Fish in *The Hotel Nantucket.* Magda bumps into Chad in line!

from *The Hotel Nantucket*

She has one more errand to run—the Nantucket Meat & Fish Market. Magda wants to get soft-shell crabs; she'll sauté them in brown butter and serve them with dirty rice and roasted asparagus. The market is pleasantly chilly and smells like coffee; it houses the only Starbucks concession on the island. Magda heads for the bounty of the long, refrigerated butcher case, where she finds impeccable trays of rib eyes, individual beef Wellingtons, steak tips in three different marinades, chicken breasts stuffed with spinach and cheese, plump rainbows of vegetable kebabs, baby back ribs, lamb chops, lobster tails, jumbo shrimp cocktails, cilantro-lime salmon, and swordfish steaks as thick as paperback books. The line at the case is four or five people long but Magda doesn't mind waiting. It's the first time she's stopped moving all day.

167Raw is *the* place I get my fish. The sign above the counter reads ANYONE WHO ASKS "IS THE FISH FRESH?" MUST GO TO THE END OF THE LINE. I've been coming here since I bought my first house in 1998. Along with the freshest and most beautiful fish, the shop sells home-made smoked bluefish pâté and key lime pies. There's a food truck in the parking lot, but we'll get to that later! Website: 167raw.com; Instagram: @167raw_nantucket.

Hatch's is my go-to liquor store; it's on Orange Street, across from **Marine Home Center.** It has everything at the most reasonable prices. Period. Website: Ackhatchs.com; Instagram: @ackhatchs.

Who's Hungry?

Nantucket is a foodie paradise. Once again, there are too many places to mention so I'm going to give you my very favorites. I won't tell you what to order (yes, I will).

SIT-DOWN LUNCH AND/OR DINNER

Sandbar**: If you're coming to Nantucket for a week or only a day, I *highly* recommend Sandbar. It's located at Jetties Beach, which is less than a mile from town and can be easily walked (you'll work up an appetite!). Sandbar was the inspiration for the Oystercatcher in my novel *Golden Girl.* It's a true beach shack with open-air indoor seating and outdoor feet-in-the-sand seating. The menu is casual—fish tacos, burgers, an outstanding chicken sandwich—and there is often live music. The bar and raw bar scene are lively, including a great buck-a-shuck in the midafternoon, but it's also very family-friendly. This is a must-visit. Website: Jettiessandbar.com; Instagram: @sandbarjetties.

The Oystercatcher (aka Sandbar) also figures prominently in my novel *Swan Song.*

from *Swan Song*

Their first stop is the Oystercatcher for buck-a-shuck. This is, in Kacy's opinion, the best way to spend the golden hour. They order two glasses of rosé and a dozen fifth points from their bartender, Carson Quinboro (a legendary Nantucket badass), who directs them to two stools overlooking the scene on Jetties Beach—striped umbrellas and sandcastles, mothers chasing after little kids with bottles of sunscreen. A cover band called Cranberry Alarm Clock plays an acoustic version of "Single Ladies," which is a little weird but also sort of charming. And, in their case, it's appropriate. Kacy raises her glass. "To all the single ladies."

Galley Beach** (aka the Blue Bistro): This is another on-the-beach setting, though one that is quite elevated.

The Galley is quintessential Nantucket. In the late sixties, it was a burger shack (there's a scene set here in my novel *Summer of '69*), but in the intervening decades, its atmosphere and food have become more refined. It has unparalleled sunset views; by tradition, when the sun sets each night, everyone in the restaurant applauds. (There are dozens of times every summer when I'll see a breathtaking sunset and say out loud, "They're clapping at the Galley.") My controversial opinion is this: Go for lunch or cocktails, not dinner. Dinner is always crowded and is a bit of a "scene." The cocktail hour can be a bit of a scene as well, but worth it because of the sunset. However, there is *no better place* on Nantucket to have an elegant sit-down lunch than the Galley. The food is fantastic. It's glamorous. It's the good life. The other perk is the view of the green, yellow, and blue umbrellas lined up at the neighboring property, Cliffside Beach Club. Website: Galleybeach.net; Instagram: @galleybeach.

There is a fun scene from *The Five-Star Weekend* that takes place at Galley Beach during lunch.

from *The Five-Star Weekend*

The best table at Galley Beach is the round six-top in the corner closest to the sand, known as Table 20. To those of us eating lunch at the Galley at noon on Sunday, it comes as no surprise that this table is where Hollis Shaw and her stars are seated. The ladies are all wearing pink or orange or both, which brings a splash of summer color to the already stunning aesthetic of the restaurant.

The Galley is open-air with white tablecloths and rattan captain's chairs. There's a zinc bar and, on the beach, a lounging area with chaises and fireplace tables. To the left is the pleasing vista of the Cliffside Beach Club, with its iconic blue, green, and canary-yellow umbrellas in neat rows and five blue Adirondack chairs sheltered by a pavilion.

The art in the Galley is eclectic, and so is the clientele. This is where the celebrities come (though we pretend not to notice them).

"This place is divine," Gigi says. "I feel like I'm in St. Tropez."

Tatum has always thought the Galley was as pretentious as South Beach, but now that she's here, she feels differently. She is, once again, sitting next to Dru-Ann, who is on her phone. Tatum can't help but peek at her screen, wondering what could be more intriguing than the views at the Galley. She sees some dude in a visor standing in the fog making a golf putt. Whatever.

"Shall we get champagne?" Hollis says. She calls over their server, Louis, and orders a magnum of Veuve Clicquot. She wants to celebrate—they're at the best table at the Galley, on the beach, on a glorious summer Sunday. They're all wearing their pink and orange. Although Dru-Ann looks smoking hot in a fuchsia bodycon dress, the fashion winner is probably Brooke, who's wearing an off-the-shoulder pink-and-orange paisley cover-up with a pom-pom fringe.

After Louis presents the magnum and pops the cork (Hollis senses the whole restaurant sneaking peeks at their table), Hollis lifts her flute. "Cheers, friends," she says. "Happy Sunday."

The Proprietors: Some things I love about the Proprietors: the long bar (thirteen seats), the creative food (outrageously delicious), the shared high-top table behind the bar and the nook by the fireplace, and the wallpaper in the bathroom. The cocktails are all handcrafted and next-level. Website: Proprietorsnantucket.com; Instagram: @propsbar.

There's a great scene in *The Hotel Nantucket* that takes place at the Proprietors. It's where Lizbet goes to meet JJ. It's their "spot," and it may very well become yours!

from *The Hotel Nantucket*

Lizbet and JJ's spot is the Proprietors on India Street. On Saturday nights in the off-season, the bartender, Tenacious Leigh, would save them the two stools at the end of the bar. Lizbet hasn't set foot in the Proprietors in months, and although she's ambivalent about meeting JJ (it's a meeting, not a date, she tells herself), she feels only joy when she strolls down the brick sidewalk to the white clapboard house, built in 1800, and opens the lipstick-red door.

Hello, old friend, she thinks. The restaurant's interior is one of her very favorites. There are refurbished wide-plank floors, exposed brick, Edison pendant lights, and a long, white-oak bar with a pressed-tin front. On the walls hang displays of mismatched china and a collection of antique door escutcheons; on the tables are mason jars filled with Nantucket wildflowers and flour-sack napkins with sage-green stripes. Lizbet almost left the Proprietors out of the Blue Book because she never wants the bar to become a place that's three deep with tourists ordering Cape Codders. In the end, she tucked it into the fine-dining section, calling it "eclectic," a place for people who want a "thoughtful dining experience and the most creative cocktails on the island."

The Nantucket Tap Room: The Tap Room at the historic Jared Coffin House has a "secret burger"—a Big Mac–esque patty melt—that isn't on the menu. It comes with outstanding french fries. Also, the popovers are a must.

This restaurant has both indoor and outdoor seating. Website: Nantuckettaproom.com; Instagram: @acktaproom.

The Nautilus**: The only thing I don't love about the Nautilus is that you need to be as wily, tireless, and determined as Indiana Jones to get a reservation. If you can meet that difficult challenge, everything will be delicious and the crowd will be lively and very attractive. My favorite dish is the blue crab fried rice (I order it with two eggs) and I count their chicken frites as, perhaps, the best dish on the entire island. This is where the women from *The Five-Star Weekend* eat on Saturday night; if Hollis chose it, you should too. Website: Thenautilus.com; Instagram: @nautilusnantucket.

Cru**: Cru sits at the end of Straight Wharf and has a lot of fun outdoor seating that attracts an extremely beautiful and bon vivant crowd. Inside there are three seating areas: front room, middle room, and back bar. I nearly always eat at the back bar, and I nearly always order the lobster roll and fries with mayo. Cru has the best raw bar scene on the island, which is saying a LOT. Cru has the appeal of see-and-be-seen, with delicious, carefully prepared food, overwater views, and excellent service (the bar staff is unparalleled!). Website: Crunantucket.com; Instagram: @crunantucket.

Cru appears in a few of my novels, including *Golden*

Girl. In lieu of Vivi's funeral service, Amy and Lorna go day-drinking to honor Vivi's life.

from *Golden Girl*

Amy asks for the day of Vivi's funeral service off and so does Lorna, claiming that she needs to support her friend, and thankfully, Wednesdays are slow at the salon. Brandi, the receptionist, reluctantly takes them off the schedule, thinking they will be attending Vivi's service.

Instead, the two of them head to Cru, located on the end of Straight Wharf, which is the best place for day-drinking on Nantucket.

They settle in at the back bar and order a bottle of champagne, the Pol Roger, "in honor of Vivi." They also order a dozen oysters and, what the hell, while they're at it, the caviar service—osetra, with all the trimmings. When the glass doors swing open, diners have an unimpeded view across the water. There's a narrow strip of boardwalk around the back bar, and Amy knows that plenty of people have fallen in; she used to hear the ruckus when she worked across the way at the Cork with JP. The ocean is spangled with sunlight; boats are tilting from side to side in the nearby slips; the ferry's horn sounds, and seagulls cry out like jealous girls. Tommy the bartender pops the cork on their bottle of champagne.

"Celebrating, ladies?" he asks.

Straight Wharf Fish Market**: This is a new Elin favorite and an absolute can't-miss. For almost as long as I've been living on Nantucket and until recently, Straight Wharf Fish Market was exactly that—a fish market. I always went there to buy my smoked bluefish pâté (theirs is the best on the island, hands down). The fish market has now been transformed into both a takeaway spot and an incredibly charming sit-down restaurant with over-water views.

I can't even decide what I love best about this place: is it the blackened swordfish sandwich, is it watching the ferries pull into the dock, is it the incredible service, or is it that I can grab a container of the bluefish pâté to go on my way out? Maybe it's the butterscotch and key lime puddings? No matter—this is a TOP recommendation. It is perfect for a day-trip lunch or a casual dinner; you can grab fried clams to go before you hop back on the ferry.

I'm only sorry I've retired from my Nantucket novels before setting a scene here! Website: Straightwharffish .com; Instagram: @straightwharffish.

The Pearl and **The Boarding House:** The Pearl was sold to new owners in 2023. While the interior has had a refresh, many of the Pearl favorites remain on the menu—two of my go-to items are the lobster rangoons and the wok-fried lobster. There are two private dining spaces above the restaurant that are ideal for private dinner parties.

Next door, the Boarding House has one of my favorite bars on the island, with a delicious burger; the menu from the Pearl is often available here as well. Downstairs is a speakeasy called **Below the Rose,** which is a very bougie, chic cocktail spot that is, as of this writing, a private club. I have been lucky enough to go there for drinks twice—this space is fabulous! Website: Pearlnantucket .com; Instagram: @pearlnantucket.

Bar Yoshi: Bar Yoshi was new in 2021; the food is light and fresh and the space appealing. This is *the* place to go for sushi, and they also offer fried rice, dumplings, and spring rolls. The restaurant is on Old South Wharf and has water views out the large open windows. Website: Bar-yoshi.com; Instagram: @baryoshinantucket.

Bar Yoshi is where Lizbet meets Heidi Bick in my novel *The Hotel Nantucket.*

from *The Hotel Nantucket*

Lizbet and Heidi meet at Bar Yoshi on Old South Wharf. They're seated at a high-top by the windows that overlook the harbor. The restaurant has a spare, chic vibe with lots of light wood, a floating glass-fronted cabinet that holds the liquor bottles, and excellent woven-basket light fixtures. Lizbet loves this place; she plans to completely overdo it on the sushi.

Or, the Whale: Or, the Whale, which is the subtitle of Melville's *Moby-Dick,* occupies prime real estate on Main Street. It has a long bar and outdoor seating in its back courtyard. A few years ago, I discovered the best reason to go to OTW: the Korean pork butt. It's expensive, but it will feed four people with leftovers to take home. This is a pork butt roasted for hours so that it is so tender and succulent you can eat it with a spoon, and it's served with light, bright, and spicy sides—lettuce wraps, fresh mint, chili sauce.

Or, the Whale also throws some seriously fun parties during the big weekends on Nantucket. I have been lucky enough to go to a DJ drag brunch there on the Sunday of **Daffodil Weekend**—it remains one of the most memorable times I've ever had on Main Street! Website: Otwnantucket.com; Instagram: @orthewhalenantucket.

Ventuno: If dining out for you means Italian food, you want to go to Ventuno, located in the heart of downtown. During my first twenty years on the island, this was the beloved restaurant 21 Federal that appears in many of my novels, including *The Blue Bistro* and *28 Summers.* The antique building has remained the same but the cuisine has changed to upscale Italian, including the best steak on the island. However, what I love best about Ventuno is the bar scene. Revelers might prefer the spirited "back bar," but I can be found at the inside bar with legendary bartender Johnny B. Sometimes you want to go where everybody knows your name. Website: Ventunorestaurant.com; Instagram: @ventunorestaurant.

Ventuno is the restaurant where Chief Kapenash and the Castaways celebrate his retirement dinner in *Swan Song*—so you know it's good.

from *Swan Song*

For tonight's dinner, Ed chose Ventuno, a restaurant housed in one of the historic residences downtown, and Andrea reserved the entire upstairs for them.

They ascend a narrow wooden staircase and find their table draped with white linen and lit by candles near the windows that overlook the charming brick sidewalks of Federal Street. All their guests have already arrived.

Ed takes his seat at the oval table and reminds himself to appreciate the things that Andrea accuses him of missing: the crystal wineglasses, the low centerpiece of dahlias and roses, the fact that Eric has worn a tie without being asked. The air smells of garlic and herbs; Tony Bennett croons in the background. This is exactly the evening Ed wanted — and yet he can't help but feel melancholy. The summer is ending, and so is his career.

After Addison assesses the wine list — it's long been his job to serve as their sommelier — he catches Ed's eye over the top of the menu.

"There's no time to get in your feelings, Ed," he says. "A bold yet subtle Barolo awaits."

The wine, Ed has to admit, tastes divine even to his unsophisticated palate (left to his own devices, he's a beer drinker), though he holds himself to half a glass. What he's really interested in tonight is food. Andrea is seated next to him but she's whispering with Phoebe and Delilah about the Richardsons. *They couldn't leave it alone; they had to one-up us!*

The Chief is going to use his wife's obsession with the Richardsons to his advantage. He does some ordering for the table—two fritto mistos, the farfalle with crab and local corn (sourced from Jeffrey and Delilah's farm), the strozzapreti with sausage and broccoli rabe, the ricotta crostini, the stuffed clams.

"Ed," Andrea says in a warning tone. Andrea is the police chief now, at least where Ed's diet is concerned.

Ed throws in an order of the giardiniera and a Caesar salad. He waits until Andrea turns away, then says to the server, "For the main course, the Fiorentina." This is the finest steak on the island; Ed dreams about it the way some men dream about Margot Robbie. It's a thirty-three-ounce porterhouse served with roasted rosemary potatoes. Ed pushes away thoughts of the salt, the fat, his heart. At home, it's been chicken, fish, and vegetables for the past six months.

When the steak arrives sizzling on the platter—the scent is enough to bring Ed to his knees—he helps himself to two rosy-pink pieces. This might be what kills him, but what a way to go.

Òran Mór: Tucked up a flight of stairs across from the **Nantucket Yacht Club** (aka the Field & Oar Club) you'll find a charming fine-dining spot called Òran Mór (Gaelic for "great song"). I used to frequent this restaurant in the 1990s, when it was called the Second Story, and then again in the 2000s, when Òran Mór was owned by different people and featured a phenomenal all-day Sunday brunch. It took a while for me to return, but now that I have, I'm a devoted fan. Òran Mór might be home to the most beautiful bar on the island. It's a bejeweled horseshoe and, if I have my way, I eat either there or at one of the few tables in the bar area, although the rest of the restaurant is delightful as well—it's the second floor of an antique building, with cozy rooms and creaky floors. The food—and cocktails—are outstanding. People rave about the Flaming Daisy, a tequila libation that comes with a spicy ice cube. My personal favorite item on the dinner menu is the smoked half chicken with white BBQ sauce and pimento cheese grits, but the duck is hard to pass up. Website: Oranmorbistro.com; Instagram: @oranmorbistro.

The Brotherhood of Thieves**: The Brotherhood is Nantucket's version of TGI Fridays, and I mean that in the best possible way. You enter on the ground floor, which has the feel of a grotto—there are brick walls with scarred wooden tables tucked into alcoves and there's a fireplace next to a long bar. This is where you go when you want to order a bowl of chowder and a lobster BLT or a plate of nachos or a really, really good burger with curly fries. The Brotherhood changed hands a few years ago and the second floor was renovated to include the **Cisco Surf Bar** on one side and the **Notch Whiskey Bar** on the other side. The Cisco Surf Bar is light and bright, with surfboards and Lauren Marttila ocean landscapes; the Notch Whiskey Bar has a moodier, more sophisticated atmosphere. You can eat on either side upstairs and the Cisco Surf Bar sometimes has live music. All in all, if you're looking for a fun, reasonably priced spot where you can get authentic Nantucket fare downtown, this is the answer. Website: Brotherhood nantucket.com; Instagram: @brotherhoodnantucket.

Straight Wharf Restaurant (not to be confused with Straight Wharf Fish Market): Straight Wharf Restaurant has a split personality. There's the bar side, which attracts a young crowd and can get loud. But the restaurant side is some of the most elegant dining on the island, the dining room is stunning, and tables on the deck are the most coveted because you can watch the ferries coming and going. (And you might catch a glimpse of *The Hotel Nantucket*'s Lizbet headed into Mario's cottage. It was while dining at Straight Wharf Restaurant that I first noticed the cottages perched at the end of a dock and thought, *I'm going to have Mario live in one of those!*) Website: Straightwharf restaurant.com; Instagram: @straightwharf.

Languedoc Bistro**: The hits keep coming! Languedoc Bistro is a classic French bistro on Broad Street. The Languedoc is elegant yet relaxed—on a crisp fall evening, you can wander in off the brick sidewalk to eat escargot in your Patagonia puffy vest (lots of people do this). I always order the cheeseburger with garlic fries; paired with the chopped salad as a starter and the Sweet Inspirations Sundae for dessert, it's the perfect meal. The downstairs dining room and the bar, helmed by the great Jimmy Jaksic, are my preferred spots, although the upstairs dining rooms are cozy and charming. I have chosen the Languedoc for my birthday dinner with my kids three times in the past few years. Website: Languedocbistro .com; Instagram: @languedocbistro.

from *Golden Girl*

A month or so before Willa and Rip's wedding, Vivi took Willa out to the Languedoc for a mother-daughter dinner. Because it was a weeknight in the spring, they were the only ones in the upstairs front room, which overlooked Broad

Street and had a view of the charming lit windows of Nantucket Bookworks.

The aesthetics of that dinner had been sheer perfection. The dining room was lit only by candles; there was a bouquet of irises on the table; the restaurant smelled of butter, garlic, veal stock, freshly baked bread. They ordered an expensive bottle of champagne and then an even more extravagant bottle of white burgundy. Willa wasn't usually all that interested in food—she would eat or drink anything you put in front of her without complaint, but she never really seemed to *enjoy* it. However, that night, she swooned over the escargot en croûte and the pan-roasted lobster with parmesan polenta, and she allowed herself to get a little tipsy.

Millie's Restaurant & Market: We've talked about Sconset, on the east end of the island, but we haven't talked yet about Madaket, on the west end. Madaket is primarily residential—a drive out to Smith's Point will take you past the tiny summer cottages (such as Wee Bit, featured in my novel *Golden Girl*). Madaket is *the* place to watch the sunset, and the vistas over Madaket Harbor will immediately elevate your Instagram. The epicenter of fun in Madaket is the Millie's universe. Millie's is probably best described as a Tex-Mex-inspired restaurant with a heavy Nantucket influence. All of the menu items are named after places on Nantucket. I always start with the Altar Rock: chips with salsa, guac, and their incredible queso. Then I move on to either the Wauwinet, which is a luscious Caesar topped with grilled shrimp and served tossed in a creamy lime dressing, or the Esther Island, a seared scallop taco with purple cabbage slaw. Millie's has a ton of outdoor seating as well as upstairs and downstairs indoor seating, but there is always a wait so I suggest going before you get too hungry. There's an ice-cream stand for after your meal, as well as a small market where you can provision for trips out to Smith's Point!

Millie's has expanded its empire to include Surfside, on the Strip just off Steamboat Wharf, and Millie's Mid-Island, at the Rotary. In addition to the usual tacos and salads, Millie's Mid-Island serves fat beach sandwiches as well as a magnificent chicken tenders box with two giant sides of honey mustard and comeback sauce. (The tenders are *delicious;* this would be the perfect way to feed a bunch of kids while the parents go enjoy a night out.) Website: Milliesnantucket.com; Instagram: @milliesnantucket.

The Chanticleer: The Chanticleer, out in Sconset, has a long-standing tradition of elegant French dining. I think it's fair to say that, back in the day, it was a bit stuffy. (For example, the original owner did not allow music in the dining room.) However, since being bought by Nantucket restaurateur Susan Handy, it has achieved the perfect balance between classic and modern. The front garden, anchored by the iconic carousel horse, is one of the most delightful places to eat in the summer. There are also two indoor dining rooms and a sunporch. (I prefer the cozy, clubby dining room to the right.) In addition to more formal French fare, there's an outstanding burger on the menu. (You may have noticed I'm a bit of a burger connoisseur.) The restaurant used to attract an older clientele, but that has completely changed—it is now popular with savvy millennials, and I am so here for it. Website: Chan ticleernantucket.com; Instagram: @chanticleernantucket.

LoLa 41**: Full disclosure: When LoLa 41 first opened, I was a frequent visitor, but then for some reason I stopped going as often. I believe the reason was because I always ordered the burger, which for many years was available from Lola Burger, at the Rotary. Once Lola Burger closed, I returned to LoLa 41, and now it's back as one of my top can't-miss recommendations. LoLa 41 is see-and-be-seen. It has low, sexy lighting and an EDM beat. The people are beautiful and it can be challenging to score a reservation. The food is absolutely *banging.* I've mentioned the Lola Burger (which comes with either regular or truffle fries), but LoLa 41 also has some of the best sushi on the island. And if you don't order the tres leches cake for dessert, you are missing out. There is a semi-private room that seats six called the Red Room, which I have booked for my annual birthday dinner with my girlfriends as well as for last-night-before-leaving-for-college dinners with my kids.

There are also LoLa outposts in Boston and Palm Beach! Website: Lola41.com; Instagram: @lola41restaurants.

Island Kitchen: Located mid-island, Island Kitchen is a charming local spot where the food is outstanding and the ice cream is even better. The ice-cream flavors change with the seasons, but in years past I have been a huge fan of the lemon soufflé and the peach and biscuits. There was a time a few years ago when my daughter was obsessed with their charcoal ice cream. (It was delicious.) Island Kitchen ice cream can also be found at the **Counter on Main Street** in Nantucket Pharmacy and at my beloved **Surfside Beach Shack.** There is no reason to stand in an outrageous line for your ice cream. Go to Island Kitchen! Website: Nantucketislandkitchen.com; Instagram: @iknantucket.

The Seagrille**: The Seagrille is a local treasure; it is impossible to walk into this restaurant (especially in the shoulder season) and not know someone (everyone). And for good reason: the food is consistently outstanding and the service is top-notch. The Seagrille is my choice for best lobster roll and best lobster bisque, and the last time I visited, they had a tater tot dish topped with caviar that was one of the best things I ate all year. There's a cool front glassed-in porch area with a lively bar, or you can sit at one of the cozy banquettes at the inside bar. You can't miss here, especially if you're looking for authentic Nantucket seafood. Website: Theseagrille.com; Instagram: @theseagrille.

GET IT TO GO!

Wicked Island Bakery: Home of the infamous morning buns. Full disclosure: In the summer of 2021, my daughter worked at Wicked Island Bakery and I heard endless sagas about the morning buns. When I dropped off my daughter, who was then age fifteen, at 6 a.m., there was already a line of people waiting for the bakery to open. One time a man saw my daughter get out of the car and then he hurried out of *his* car, because he thought she was there to get in line. It's that bad and worse. The morning buns are handcrafted cinnamon rolls that can only be made thirty at a time and take forty-five minutes. The frenzy is caused by how delicious they are, yes, but it's also the law of supply and demand in action (there is a six-bun-per-customer limit in the summer). The stories I heard about adults behaving badly in regard to the morning buns prompt me now to remind everyone that civility and kindness are always mandatory, especially when you're dealing with people in the service industry, and especially when those people are teenagers working a summer job. We adults must lead by example. Period.

Wicked Island Bakery also has *outrageously delicious* ham and cheese croissants as well as . . . the almond croissants that I used in *The Hotel Nantucket*! And it's where you can procure Amy's cookies, adorable sugar cookies decorated in any number of charming ways by #girl boss Dr. Amy Hinson. (Amy was my forensics expert for *Golden Girl*.) Website: Wickedislandbakery.com; Instagram: @wickedislandbakery.

Born & Bread**: Every Wednesday either before or after my weekly signing, I make a pilgrimage to Born & Bread for a loaf (or two) of their classic sourdough, sliced thin. (They also have, periodically, an addictive olive sourdough.) Born & Bread also offers coffee, scones, cruffins and other sweet and savory pastries, cookies, cupcakes, and incredible sandwiches, including the ABC grilled cheese! Website: Bornandbreadnantucket.com; Instagram: @bornandbreadnantucket.

from *The Hotel Nantucket*

Lizbet isn't sure where all this self-doubt is coming from; she's probably just hungry. She's tempted to run over to Born & Bread for a sandwich, but there isn't time. Her next interview is here.

The woman, Alessandra, holds out a white paper bag. "I brought you an ABC grilled cheese from Born & Bread on the off chance you've been so busy interviewing that you skipped lunch."

Lizbet's blue eyes widen. "Thank you! That was so...intuitive. I did skip lunch, and the ABC is my favorite sandwich." She accepts the bag.

Staff of five, Lizbet thinks as she takes a bite of the apple, bacon, and white cheddar grilled cheese on cranberry-studded sourdough that Alessandra brought her.

Lemon Press: Do you love fresh-pressed juices, kombucha, acai bowls, avocado toast? If yes, then you must make a visit to Main Street superstar Lemon Press. It provides a breakfast or lunch of champions—fresh, healthy, delicious. And it's female-owned and -operated! The line can be quite long; this place is super popular for a reason, so bring a book (or buy one; Mitchell's Book Corner is right across the street!). Website: Lemonpressnantucket .com; Instagram: @lemonpressnantucket.

Walter's Deli and **Stubbys:** Both Walter's and Stubbys are on the Strip, which is the block between Easy Street and Water Street that is known for inexpensive, fast, and delicious eats.

Walter's Deli is an unsung hero. They offer made-to-order hot and cold sandwiches, including the best Reuben on the island, one of the best lobster rolls (it's a bargain by Nantucket standards), and *the* best BLT I've *ever* had (classic white bread, good mayo, a pile of hot crispy bacon, local tomatoes, and lettuce). If you're stepping off or getting on the boat at Steamboat Wharf, be sure to make a pit stop at Walter's.

Stubbys has achieved icon status, especially among the under-twenty-five crowd. Think of it as McDonald's and Chick-fil-A's cooler cousin. Stubbys is known for its waffle fries, and they also have an outstanding chicken sandwich, double-double cheeseburger, and Jamaican specialties. Stubbys stays open until 2 a.m., making it a *very* popular late-night stop, and finally, this past year, some marketing genius created a hoodie that says ENDED UP AT STUBBYS. More than one of these hang in my own mudroom! Website: Stubbysnantucket.com; Instagram: @eatstubbys.

167Raw**: You saw mention of 167 earlier in the markets chapter, and now let's talk about the food truck next to the fabulous fish market. This place has the best tuna burger on the island. You can order it online and pick it up on your way to the beach. Highly recommended! You can also get fish tacos, carnitas tacos, lobster rolls, and their famous ceviche and guacamole. To order in advance, visit 167rawtakeout.com/food-truck.

Something Natural**: An island institution. It was my discovery of Something Natural herb bread in my first Nantucket summer, 1993, that made me want to move to the island. The sandwiches at Something Natural are the stuff of legend. They're huge; a whole sandwich can easily feed two people. The cookies: also huge, also legendary. Something Natural has a garden setting with picnic tables if you want to ride your bike up Cliff Road and eat there, or you can phone in an order to go and then head to the beach. My usual order is the avocado, cheddar, and chutney on herb bread, which might sound unexpected, but it tastes like summertime to me. You can buy loaves of their breads at the Cliff Road location or at Stop & Shop. My kids are partial to the Portuguese bread, which makes THE best toast, and Something Natural now offers pink salt sourdough. Website: Somethingnatural.com; Instagram: @somethingnaturalack.

from *Winter Storms*

She has asked for one thing, discreetly, as a wedding present from her three children, and that is a lunch at Something Natural, just the four of them. She thinks about how selfish it is for her to request this—no Drake, no Isabelle, no Jennifer, no grandchildren, no Kelley or Mitzi—but Margaret doesn't care. She wants an hour eating sandwiches in the sunshine with her children.

Not on Sunday, when everyone will be hungover

and exhausted. Margaret wants to spend Sunday with Drake alone. But on Monday, at noon.

They all get in line and order their sandwiches. Margaret gets the Sheila's Favorite on oatmeal; Ava gets avocado, cheddar, and chutney; Kevin orders smoked turkey, Swiss, and tomato on herb bread; Patrick gets the lobster salad on pumpernickel.

Margaret adds chips, Nantucket Nectars, and four huge chocolate chip cookies to the order.

Thai House and Siam to Go: Nantucket is lucky to have not one but two high-quality Thai restaurants. I like the spring rolls better at Thai House but I prefer the shrimp pad thai at Siam to Go. In a place that can sometimes feel wanting when it comes to authentic, inexpensive food from other cultures, I am grateful for these two spots. Websites: Ackthaihouse.com and Siamtogonantucket.com; Thai House Instagram: @thaihouse_nantucket.

The Boat House: There was a time when everyone who worked at the Boat House knew my middle child by name because he ate there every day after school. In addition to burgers and fried chicken sandwiches, the Boat House serves tacos and burritos. Everything is fresh and reasonably priced. A lot of times, if I'm going out and I have hungry kids to feed, I'll order their dinner here and everyone is thrilled. Website: Boathousenantucket.com; Instagram: @boat_house_nantucket.

Sophie T's Pizza: This has long been our family's go-to for pizza and subs. (For a stretch of maybe ten years, every sleepover birthday party involved a run to Sophie T's.) I love the ACK Mack pizza, a play on a Big Mac, with ground beef, American cheese, onions, pickles, and a sesame crust, drizzled with special sauce. It's delicious! Sophie T's is also across the street from the Chicken Box. Website: Acksophiets.com; Instagram: @sophietspizza.

from *The Five-Star Weekend*

The band plays one great song after another—the Violent Femmes, the Cure, Weezer—and the group of Chads keep Brooke's and Dru-Ann's drinks flowing. When the lights come up and the lead singer launches into "Closing Time," Dru-Ann steers Brooke around the couples who are about to hook up and out the side door—where they run smack into a ridiculously long line of people waiting for cabs.

No, Dru-Ann thinks. *This won't do.* She'll call an UberXL. Hell, she'll use Alto, the world's most expensive rideshare app. Do they have Alto on Nantucket? No, it turns out, they do not. UberXL, then—but the nearest one is thirty-seven minutes away. They should have left the bar earlier. It's past one now; at this rate, they won't make it back to Hollis's until two. Dru-Ann hits Confirm Ride because what else can she do, it's too far to walk—then she sees the pizza parlor across the street, Sophie T's, is open.

Yes! she thinks. She's *starving;* the chicken and frites at Nautilus were a lifetime ago. "Follow me," Dru-Ann says to Brooke. "We're getting a slice."

Soon Dru-Ann and Brooke are holding hot, delightfully floppy pieces of pepperoni pizza. They take their paper plates outside and sit on the curb with their legs stretched out into the parking lot.

Provisions: Conveniently located on Straight Wharf, this sandwich shop is a long-standing Nantucket tradition. It's home to the Turkey Terrific, a classic Thanksgiving sandwich that serves as the ultimate comfort food as you line up to get back on the ferry at the end of your stay. The sandwiches are fresh and made to order on locally baked bread. Instagram: @provisionsnantucket.

I Love the Nightlife, I Want to Boogie!

The Chicken Box: And now, the moment you've all been waiting for: THE CHICKEN BOX! A few things you should know: It's referred to as simply the Box. If you use the sentence "I closed the Box last night," you'll sound like a Nantucket local. Also: There is no chicken, *not one piece of chicken.* It's just a bar, the best dive bar in America, with beer-sticky floors and beautiful people three deep at the bar and terrific bands, including headliners like the Revivalists, Grace Potter, and Donavon Frankenreiter, who come (I happen to believe) because of their love of the venue. When I go, I don't mess around: I can be found in the front row dancing. The Box is the most popular event during the Elin Hilderbrand Bucket List Weekend, and it is the most visited place by people who come to the island looking for all the spots mentioned in my books. Website: Thechickenbox.com; Instagram: @theboxnantucket.

from *Beautiful Day*

Margot wandered to the back of the bar, where there were three pool tables and the crowd was thinner. The Chicken Box used to be the place she came to dance every night of the summer. When she was only nineteen, she sneaked in using her cousin's ID to see Dave Matthews play. She had seen Squeeze, and Hootie and the Blowfish, and an all-girl AC/DC tribute band called Hell's Belles, and a funk band called Chucklehead who frequented the same coffee shop that she did back in New York. Margot couldn't decide if being at the Box made her feel younger or older.

The Gaslight: Want to hear live music but don't want to leave downtown? You're in luck! The building that used to house the Starlight movie theater was reimagined a few years ago to become the Gaslight, a bar, restaurant, and live-music venue. The food is nothing short of amazing—it comes to you from Liam Mackey, the chef of the Nautilus—and at ten o'clock the music kicks in. If you need one more reason to check it out, there's also a champagne vending machine! Website: Gaslightnantucket.com; Instagram: @gaslightnantucket.

from *Golden Girl*

The Gaslight used to be a movie theater but has been reimagined as a live-music venue. It has a pressed-tin ceiling and a wall of vintage turntables and speakers; there's a stage with a hot-pink neon sign that says GASLIGHT over the drum set. The crowd at the bar is lively; the food is delicious, and the cocktails are the kind that have been created by a mixologist and include ingredients Amy has never heard of.

There's one open seat at the bar — Amy imagines this conveniently happens in Vivi's novels as well — and Amy doesn't recognize anyone, another blessing.

The bartender is a big, strapping bear of a man named Nick. He's a Nantucket celebrity. He says, "Are you waiting for someone, ma'am?"

"Yes," Amy says brightly. "My friend Lorna."

"Lorna from RJ Miller?" Nick says. "She cuts my hair. She should have texted me to let me know you were coming, I would have saved you two seats."

"May I please have a Blackout Barbie?" Amy asks. "Two, actually. I want to have one here waiting for Lorna when she arrives."

The Blackout Barbie is a cocktail made with fresh-picked strawberries from Bartlett's Farm, lemon juice, tequila, and a splash of cava; it's garnished with thyme blossoms and served with an oversize round ice cube. It's delicious. Amy drinks both hers and "Lorna's" in short order and after she asks Nick for a third, she says, "I guess Lorna isn't coming."

"Yeah, I texted her," Nick says. "She's off-island."

Amy isn't sure if she should act surprised or just keep rolling. She decides on the latter. "In that case, I'm ordering food. How about the cheese-burger bao buns and the poke nachos?"

The Club Car: The Club Car is a fine-dining restau-rant that incorporates one of the train cars from the old Nantucket Railroad as its bar, hence the name. The food at the Club Car is fresh and inventive, but the real star of the place is the sing-along piano bar. Choose your requests carefully! Plan to tip twenty bucks if you want to hear "Tiny Dancer," "Shallow," or "Piano Man." Web-site: Theclubcar.com; Instagram: @nantucketclubcar.

from *Silver Girl*

Dan pulled Connie and Meredith down the street to the Club Car. There was more champagne ordered for the ladies, while Dan drank a glass of port. Meredith was tentative at first—again, scan-ning the old Pullman car for people she knew. (On the way, Dan had told Meredith that this Pullman car had once been part of the train that ran from Nantucket town out to Sconset.) But Meredith was drawn to the back end of the car where a man played the piano and people gathered around him singing "Sweet Caroline" and "Ob-La-Di, Ob-La-Da." At one point, Meredith caught sight of Dan nuzzling Connie's neck at the bar. This was the romantic end of their date; they would both want to be rid of Meredith soon. The piano player launched into "I Guess That's Why They Call It the Blues," and Meredith belted it out, thinking of Sister Delphine at Merion Mercy, who had trained Meredith's voice for four years in the madrigal choir. Now here she was, a rather drunk torch singer.

Salons

RJ Miller Salon & Spa: This has been my salon for over eighteen years—hair, nails, facials, and spa treatments—and now my kids go here as well. It's home away from home for me; the service, professionalism, warmth, and friendliness are unparalleled. Website: Rjmillersalons.com; Instagram: @rjmillersalonspa.

Darya Salon and Spa: I love Darya! Her full-service salon can now be found at the White Elephant Hotel...right down the street from the Hotel Nantucket! Website: Daryasalonspa.com; Instagram: @daryasalonspa.

Working Out

Forme Barre Nantucket: I have stated on my social media that the best way to see me on Nantucket — other than by attending my weekly signings on Main Street — is to attend the daily 9:30 a.m. barre class at Forme during the summer. I am *consistently* there. (If I'm not there, I'm either away or dying.) After we plié together, I am happy to sign books or take pictures outside. In summertime, Forme also offers beach barre classes with the barre bus at Nobadeer Beach. I go to barre on the beach at least once per summer. (Forme also has virtual classes, which I take when I'm traveling.) Website: Formebarre.com; Instagram: @forme.nantucket.

Nantucket Cycling and Fitness: If you're looking for a spin class, this is the place! Before I bought my Peloton, this is where I would spin. The studio is tucked back off Old South Road and can be tricky to find, but once you know where it is, you'll be charmed. The space is appealing, the instructors are tough, and you will get your money's worth. Website: Nantucketfitness.com; Instagram: @nantucketcyclingfitness.

The Nantucket Hotel: The Nantucket Hotel has one of the best fitness centers on the island, and in the off-season they offer memberships to the public. They also have a magical yoga instructor in **Pat Dolloff.** Follow Pat on Instagram @patricia_dolloff.

Other Fun Stuff!

Endeavor (sailing): When you're visiting an island, nothing compares to a day out on the water. Endeavor runs three sailing cruises per day plus a sunset cruise (all weather permitting) on a thirty-one-foot Friendship sloop that was built by

Captain Jim Genthner. You can reserve spots on the boat with others or rent the entire thing for yourself. Perfect for groups — large families, bachelorette parties, girls' weekends, et cetera. You can bring your own food and drink. The *Endeavor* has seen more than its share of engagements! Website: Endeavorsailing.com; Instagram: @endeavorsailing.

from *Winter Storms*

Nathaniel is standing at the start of the Straight Wharf, just in front of the Gazebo. He's holding a bottle of Veuve Clicquot and two champagne flutes.

This time Ava feels certain the champagne is for her.

"Where are we going?" she asks.

"Follow me," he says.

He leads her down the dock to where the fishing boats are lined up and stops at the *Endeavor*. The *Endeavor* is a thirty-one-foot Friendship sloop that does charter harbor cruises, specializing in sunsets; Kelley and Mitzi recommend it for guests of the inn all the time. Ava loves seeing the boat on the horizon; she always imagines how lucky the people on board are. She hasn't been on the boat since Mitzi rented it for Kelley's fiftieth birthday.

"Are we going?" she asks Nathaniel.

"We're going," he says.

"By ourselves?"

"Just you and me, the captain, and the first mate."

Ava can't believe it. This is an extravagant gesture. In her mind, it's even better than a villa in Tuscany. Ava removes her shoes and climbs aboard with Nathaniel following. The hot day has turned into a mild evening, and because it's the longest day of the year, there's still an hour of daylight before sunset. Ava stretches out on the bow — they're the only guests; they have the whole boat to themselves! — and Nathaniel joins her. He pops the cork on the champagne and pours two glasses. They putter out of the slip and into the harbor.

Ava has lived on Nantucket since she was nine years old, but she is still dazzled every time she gets out on the water. It doesn't happen as often as one might think. She takes the ferry, of course, and on the occasional summer Sunday, she will join Shelby and Zack in their whaler for a trip to Coatue or Great Point. But given that Ava's usually at school or the inn, most of her Nantucket experience takes place on land.

The sails go up as the boat rounds Brant Point Light. There are a couple of kids on the beach collecting horseshoe crabs. Ava waves at them. The *Endeavor* sails around the jetty and out into Nantucket Sound. Ava sees the Cliffside Beach Club and the Galley restaurant. Piano music and the clink of glasses drift over the water. The sun lowers on the horizon, a ball of pink fire.

Miacomet Golf Course: As Blond Sharon intimates in *The Hotel Nantucket,* it *can* be tricky getting a tee time at Miacomet Golf Course because it's the only public eighteen-hole course on the island. Miacomet also has a very good and popular restaurant and bar, a driving range, and a putting green. Website: Miacometgolf.com; Instagram: @miacometgolfcourse.

Absolute Sport Fishing and **Bill Fisher Outfitters:** For all my Angler Cupcakes out there! Eric Kapenash in *Swan Song* runs a fictional fishing charter on a fictional boat called *Beautiful Day* (see what I did there?), but in real life I am friendly with the captains of these two charter fishing businesses, and you'll be in good hands. Charming and professional. Websites: Absolutesportfishing.com and Billfishertackle.com; Instagrams: @absolutesportfishingack and @billfishertackle.

Holidays and Festivals

Daffodil Weekend (the last weekend in April; dates vary): Daffodil Weekend (aka Daffy; used in a sentence: "Are you coming for Daffy?") kicks off the unofficial "season" on Nantucket.

The stores in town reopen, the ferries fill up with people wearing yellow and green, and you start seeing a lot of classic cars trundling over the cobblestones of Main Street. Daffodil Weekend began in the mid-1970s when the Nantucket Garden Club sponsored a flower show. Two years later, garden club member Jean MacAusland started an initiative to plant one million daffodil bulbs across Nantucket. Today, there are over two million daffodils on Nantucket, and the island celebrates their blooming with not only a flower show but also an antique-car parade that starts in town and travels out the Milestone Road to Sconset. The cars often have themes — Renoir's Boating Party, for example. Once in Sconset, the cars park along Main Street and set up elaborate tailgate picnics.

from *28 Summers*

The end of April brings the Daffodil Festival. This is the first big weekend of the year, the official start of the season on Nantucket. There's a classic-car parade out to Sconset where everyone gathers to tailgate. Scott enters the Blazer in the parade and says he'll decorate the car if Mallory will handle the theme and the picnic. Mallory and Apple come up with *The Official Preppy Handbook* as the theme — "Look, Muffy, a book for us" — and Mallory pulls out the Baltimore Junior League cookbook that Kitty gave her several Christmases ago to find recipes for their preppy picnic.

Mallory can't believe how great the Blazer looks when Scott is finished with it. It has a blanket of daffodils on the hood and a cute daffodil wreath on the grille. It's a sunny day, though chilly, but they decide to drive out to Sconset with the top down. Scott and Hugo sit up front in their navy blazers and pink oxford shirts and Mallory and Apple and Link and Roxanne sit in the back. Apple is wearing a white turtleneck and a navy cardigan, and Mallory has on a yellow Fair Isle sweater and the Bean Blucher moccasins she's owned since high school. Link is in a polo shirt with the collar popped. They wave at the spectators on the side of Milestone Road, and Roxanne barks; she has on a collar printed with navy whales.

They get to Sconset and set up their picnic: gin and tonics, tea sandwiches, boiled asparagus spears, deviled eggs, tiny weenies in barbecue sauce. The judges come by and spend a long time admiring the fine detail on the sandwiches; they take note of the outfits, Apple's grosgrain watchband, Scott's tortoiseshell Jack Kennedy sunglasses. Mallory catches a glimpse of herself in the side-view mirror. In her sweater and pearl earrings, she looks alarmingly like Kitty. A photographer from the *Inquirer and Mirror* snaps a picture of Mallory and Scott in front of the Blazer. Scott tells the reporter the story about how he sold Mallory the Blazer back in the summer of 1993 and how they met ten years later and are now dating.

They win first prize for their tailgate and an honorable mention for the Blazer.

The entire weekend is festive. Don't miss the Flower Power Party at the Nantucket Whaling Museum, sponsored by the Nantucket Historical Association, or the drag brunch with DJ on Sunday at Or, the Whale. Cisco Brewers is also popping over Daffy. This is one of my favorite weekends of the year! I celebrate by making June Johnsen's recipe for ribbon sandwiches.

Ribbon Sandwiches

(Recipe from June Swift Johnsen, longtime Nantucketer)

A ribbon sandwich is essentially a tri-layered finger sandwich whose colors evoke strips of ribbon.

- ✦ 4 hard-boiled eggs
- ✦ 1 teaspoon white sugar
- ✦ 1 teaspoon yellow mustard
- ✦ 2–3 tablespoons mayonnaise
- ✦ salt and pepper
- ✦ 1 bunch minced scallions (green and light-green parts)
- ✦ 2 eight-ounce containers Philadelphia plain whipped cream cheese
- ✦ ½ cup coarsely chopped maraschino cherries
- ✦ 1 teaspoon maraschino juice
- ✦ 2 loaves Pepperidge Farm thin-sliced white bread with the crusts cut off (it *must* be thin-sliced bread!)

Prepare three colored fillings: For the yellow filling (egg salad), mash the eggs well until the yolks are powder and the whites are in tiny pieces. Add the sugar, yellow mustard, and mayonnaise. Salt and pepper to taste. For the green filling (scallion cream cheese), add the minced scallions to one container of cream cheese and stir until well mixed. For the pink filling (cherry cream cheese), add the maraschino cherries and maraschino juice to one container of cream cheese and stir until well blended.

Arrange four slices of the Pepperidge Farm bread on a clean cutting board. Spread one slice with the egg salad, one with the scallion cream cheese, and one with the cherry cream cheese, stacking them and topping with a final slice of bread. Using a serrated knife, carefully slice the sandwich into three equal rectangles. When you separate them, they should show the three colors of the fillings. Continue until all the bread is gone. Cover with plastic wrap or store in Tupperware until ready to serve.

Figawi (Memorial Day weekend): Are you older than thirty? Skip Figawi.

Figawi (the name reputedly comes from sailors who were lost in the fog and shouted out, "Where the f*ck are we?") is technically a sailing race—but over the years it has devolved into a weekend when people in their twenties come bearing thirty-packs of Bud Light with the goal of drinking as much as they can for as long as they can. Figawi is such a blight on the island that every Memorial Day weekend, I hope for rain...and I am not alone.

from *The Rumor*

He had a love-hate relationship with Memorial Day weekend. On the one hand, he couldn't wait for it to arrive, announcing, as it did, the start of summer.

However, Memorial Day on Nantucket also meant Figawi, a Nantucket tradition that only grew bigger and more obnoxious every year. It was, ostensibly, a sailing race from Hyannis to Nantucket and back again. The genesis of the name was everyone's favorite fact about the weekend. One year, while sailing in dense fog, some old salt called out, "Hey, where the figawi?" And in this way, the race was named. Because, really—who doesn't love sanctioned profanity?

Figawi weekend had morphed in recent years from a sailing race to a drinking race. It was a contest of who could drink the most, who could drink the fastest, who could stay up drinking the latest, who could get up the earliest and start drinking, who could act like the biggest jerk (this was the nicest term Eddie could come up with, although he had dozens at his disposal) while drinking. Figawi was popular with the post-collegiate crowd—kids who had just graduated from Hamilton or Bowdoin or Middlebury or, Eddie's least favorite, Boston College. ("How do you know if somebody went to BC?" he liked to quip. "They'll tell you.") These kids now had jobs in Manhattan or Boston as editorial assistants or Wall Street grunts or preschool teachers, or they were in law school at NYU or medical school at Harvard. They lived in apartments in the West Village or the Back Bay that their parents still paid for, but in general, they were trying to be adults. They met for drinks after work on Newbury Street or in SoHo, they skipped church on Sundays and brunched instead, and on summer weekends they "went away."

Figawi weekend on Nantucket was made for them. The men wore their faded red shorts from Murray's; they tied cable-knit sweaters around their necks, they wore sunglasses inside because they were so dreadfully hungover. The girls—or, rather, *women*—paraded around in patio dresses without underwear. They all thought they were Diane von Furstenberg by the Beverly Hills Hotel pool in 1973. And they all carried handbags that seemed to contain as much crap as a thirty-gallon Hefty bag. Eddie wanted to tell them that they could go on *Let's Make a Deal* with all the stuff they had in their purses—but they would have had no idea what he was talking about! Certain women, however, wore outfits that looked like they'd been stolen from the trailer-park clothesline—cutoff jean shorts and tight T-shirts that said SORRY FOR PARTYING.

The women irked Eddie more than the men, probably because he had daughters.

If the weather was sunny, the Figawians—truly their own nation—funneled down Hummock Pond Road in their rental Jeeps with cases of Bud Light in the back. The beaches were patrolled by rent-a-cops on ATVs who had a field day issuing tickets for public consumption and littering. The red-suited lifeguards pulled people out of the ocean left and right because the riptide was notoriously bad in May, and no matter how educated these young bucks were ("bucks" substituted for dozens of other terms Eddie had at his disposal), they didn't seem to know that the way to get out of the rip was to swim parallel to shore until the grip of the waves let them go.

But this year, there was rain.

Rain on Figawi weekend was a thousand times worse than sun on Figawi because the activities of beaching and drinking were replaced by drinking and drinking. The epicenter of Figawi drinking was always the Straight Wharf—specifically, the Tavern, the Gazebo, the eponymous Straight Wharf Restaurant, and Cru. These restaurants were bursting at their seersucker and madras seams with screaming, laughing, swearing, hiccuping, posturing nouveau adults who were only just learning how to appreciate a good Bloody Mary and suck down an oyster without dripping onto their Brooks Brothers.

The Nantucket Book Festival (mid-June): I'm obviously not impartial, but as a person who has attended book festivals across the country, I can say that the Nantucket

Book Festival is…elevated. The festival is diverse and inclusive, it's well-run, and the discussions, parties, and activities are all organic to the island. For years, I experienced major FOMO because I would always be away on tour while the festival was held. (But no longer! Now I plan to not only participate but attend as a regular citizen.) To support the fes-

tival, we throw an Elin-themed party at the Nantucket Hotel the first week of August. Keep your eyes peeled for the announcement! Website: Nantucketbookfestival.org; Instagram: @nantucketbookfestival.

The Nantucket Film Festival (mid-June, but after the book festival): The NFF was founded in 1997 and from the beginning has been focused on screenwriting. It is low-key as far as film festivals go, though celebrities do come to Nantucket for it. The films are screened at both the Dreamland Theater and the Sconset Casino, and there are plenty of talks as well, some at glorious private homes around the island. Website: Nantucketfilmfestival .org; Instagram: @nantucketfilmfestival.

The Fourth of July: The Fourth of July is a big deal on

Nantucket. On the morning of the Fourth, there are a host of patriotic activities downtown: a bike parade up Main Street, a pie-eating contest, and the infamous water fight with the Nantucket Fire Department. On the evening of July fifth, Nantucket Visitor Services sponsors fireworks, and thousands of people crowd onto Jetties Beach with their chairs, blankets, and picnic baskets.

Nobadeer Beach, on the south shore, is the beach of choice for revelry during the day on the Fourth — again, if you're over thirty, you might want to check out one of the other beaches I've suggested in this guide!

I have written about the Fourth countless times in my novels (in my book *Summer People,* a young character gets lost on Jetties Beach in the aftermath of the fireworks), but my favorite scene takes place in my novel *Swan Song.*

from *Swan Song*

The Chief is restless. The Fourth is one of his least favorite days of the year. It starts with all of the antics out at Nobadeer Beach — girls going topless, guys doing flips off the dunes, idiots using empty beer bottles as projectiles, the entire Boston

College offensive line getting into a scrap with half the Morgan Stanley trading floor. Every year the Chief's officers write over a hundred tickets for underage drinking. This segues right into fifteen thousand people cramming onto Jetties Beach with their hibachi grills and open containers. Talk about a public-safety nightmare. Then there are the bozos who have bought fireworks out of state and choose to set them off from their buddy's widow's walk. There are noise complaints, people losing fingers, yards catching on fire.

Boston Pops on Nantucket (second Saturday in August): My personal favorite "holiday" on Nantucket benefits Nantucket Cottage Hospital. The Boston Pops at Jetties Beach began in the mid-1990s—and the evening raises upwards of two million dollars for our island hospital, a cause near and dear to my heart. This is the hospital where I gave birth to three of my children, and it's also where I was diagnosed with breast cancer.

The Pops concert takes place on Jetties Beach—people pack picnics and sit in the sand while the Boston Pops performs. In recent years, they've included a special guest—we've had Carly Simon, Kenny Loggins, the Spinners—or a tribute band, such as Super Diamond. The show ends with a magnificent drone show. In the summer of 2024, I was honored to serve as the host for the night!

Halloween: Nantucket really does Halloween right — especially if you have kids! Main Street closes for a costume parade, led by the Nantucket town crier, and all of the stores hand out candy (good candy!). There's also a haunted house at the old fire station.

Thanksgiving: Thanksgiving on Nantucket has traditionally been celebrated by the Turkey Plunge at Children's Beach, which benefits the **Nantucket Atheneum** (our public library). Yes, people go into the water, no matter the weather. (Full disclosure: I have never done it.) The other major Nantucket Thanksgiving celebration is the annual tree lighting downtown. Nantucket's streets are lined with Christmas trees that will later be decorated by classes at the elementary school. At five o'clock there's a short ceremony and then the switch is flipped, and all the trees light up at once. We sometimes have visiting dignitaries for this!

A new Thanksgiving tradition, as of 2023, is the stage play *Elin Hilderbrand's Winter Street,* put on by **Theatre Workshop of Nantucket.** Theatre Workshop director Justin Cerne wrote a delightful adaptation of my four Winter Street novels, turning them into a two-hour play. The production starts running the week of Thanksgiving and continues into Stroll (see below). If you love the Quinn family, you will be overjoyed by this production. Theatre Workshop of Nantucket has secured exclusive rights to this play so that it can run every holiday season in perpetuity. It's a can't-miss**!

Christmas Stroll: The biggest holiday in the off-season and possibly all year is the Nantucket Chamber of Commerce's Christmas Stroll (known simply as Stroll; used in a sentence: "Elin is signing at four thirty the Saturday of Stroll"). We already know that the trees are lit, and as you might guess, the shop windows are decorated with classic elegance (think antique sleds; there are no plastic candy canes here). The Killen family places a lit Christmas tree in a dory at the Easy Street Boat Basin. (Did you even *go* to Stroll if you didn't photograph the Killen dory?) Traditionally, the Nantucket Historical Association throws a benefit party to preview their Festival of Trees display in the Nantucket Whaling Museum. This is my favorite party of the year; I describe this party in, you guessed it, my novel *Winter Stroll.* The Festival of Trees exhibit is open to the public through the year's end and should not be missed—businesses and creative islanders decorate trees that are displayed throughout the museum.

On Saturday of Stroll, Main Street closes. Santa arrives on a Coast Guard vessel at noon, and after he's escorted up Main Street by the Nantucket town crier, children can visit with Santa in the Methodist church. There are Victorian carolers. There's a food tent in the Stop & Shop parking lot at the bottom of Main Street. In years of yore, you would see ladies in fur coats. Now people tend to dress up as Buddy from *Elf* and the Grinch and naughty Mrs. Claus. There are book signings at Mitchell's throughout the day (my signing is traditionally the final one of the day, at four thirty). There are live bands at Cisco Brewers. Not every restaurant is open so it's very important to make dinner reservations way in advance—most restaurants start taking these reservations after Columbus Day.

One of my readers, Jenna T. from Jacksonville, Florida, compiled a super-helpful list of Stroll tips. She mentions getting the "Stroll scarf"—there's a new scarf created every year for sale, and the official one can only be purchased at the Nantucket Boat Basin Authentic Shop. Jenna recommends B-ACK Yard BBQ on Straight Wharf as a great place to get drinks as you watch for Santa's arrival. She and her crew had lunch at the Corner Table, a lovely spot for sandwiches, pastries, prepared foods, and coffee. Jenna loved the front porch of the

Nantucket Hotel for drinks and the indoor restaurant **Breeze** for lunch or dinner.

Jenna recommends booking your hotel early and reminded me that, like at the Hotel Nantucket, there is a three-night minimum over Stroll.

The proper greeting is "Happy Stroll!" Thanks, Jenna!

Giving Back

If you've visited Nantucket, you've already done your share by plumping the local economy with your hard-earned dollars. (And as you've learned: Nantucket is NOT cheap!) However, if you're inclined to give even more, I will share my favorite Nantucket-based nonprofits. The three places I'm suggesting are extremely beneficial to the year-round community, including the workforce who cleaned your rooms, washed your dishes, pruned the hedges, and picked up the trash.

The Nantucket Boys & Girls Club**: I sat on the board of directors at the Boys & Girls Club for nine years and chaired their summer benefit for three. (Fodder for my novel *A Summer Affair*!) The Club is my number one nonprofit because without a safe place for people to send their children after school, the island would grind to a halt. The Club underwent a massive renovation and is now a leader among its peers—not only the building itself but the programming. They have just initiated their own preschool as well as offering a summer camp, a full slate of after-school activities, and a year-round sports program. If you donate to the Club, you will be directly helping all of working Nantucket. Website: Nantucketboysandgirls club.org; Instagram: @nantucketbgc.

The Nantucket Booster Club: All of our student athletes (including, back in the day, my own children) have to travel on the fast ferry to get to their away games. This costs money, as does ground transportation on the other side. If you're a person who's passionate about youth sports, then donating to the Boosters might be for you. Website: Nantucketboosterclub.com.

Nantucket Food, Fuel, and Rental Assistance**: People tend to misunderstand Nantucket as an island populated solely by wealthy people. This perception belies the fact that there is an enormous population of islanders who work in the service industry or trades or in seasonal businesses where regular work dries up in the cold winter months. The NFFRA—which includes the **Nantucket Food Pantry**—has long been addressing the needs of our islanders with food insecurity. In recent years, they have distributed over twenty thousand bags of groceries to vulnerable families. Website: Assistnantucket.org.

I featured the NFFRA in my final Nantucket novel, *Swan Song*.

from *Swan Song*

"I'll leave you alone," Andrea says, touching Kacy's shoulder. She grabs the last bottle of champagne from the fridge and gets back to the deck in time to hear Delilah say, "If the Richie Richardsons want to get involved in the community, they should donate to the food pantry."

Yes! Andrea thinks. Delilah's on the board of Nantucket Food, Fuel, and Rental Assistance. Everyone thinks of Nantucket as a wealthy enclave, but there's an underserved community — service workers, day laborers, many of them foreign nationals — who struggle with the insane rents and high cost of absolutely everything, especially in the desolate off-season.

On behalf of Nantucket, I thank you for even reading this section! It's my mission to donate or contribute in meaningful ways to as many Nantucket nonprofits as possible.

"Best for . . ." Suggestions

Here, for the first time, are some of my thoughts on specific itineraries!

ARE YOU THROWING A BACHELORETTE PARTY?

The best time for a large group to visit the island is during the shoulder season. For bachelorette parties, I suggest mid-May to mid-June (but skip Memorial Day weekend—trust me!). The fall is lovely midweek, though the weekends are often booked up with weddings.

You'll all want to stay together, so I'd suggest renting a house (excellent real estate agencies include **Island Properties Nantucket, Congdon & Coleman Real Estate,** and **Great Point Properties**) or getting suites at the Nantucket Hotel.

By all means, schedule a group barre class at Forme Barre Nantucket; you may bump into the author of this book. You can pop next door afterward for a coffee or treat from Pip and Anchor, or you can stroll down to Nantucket Meat & Fish Market to pick up marinated salmon to grill for dinner.

See if you can score the Captain's Table at the Nautilus one night for dinner. Other suggestions: the Red Room at LoLa 41, one of the private upstairs rooms at the Pearl, or the party room at Slip 14.

You will want to spend one afternoon at Cisco Brewers. A group lunch at Galley Beach is also highly recommended.

You can also call Nantucket Catering Company, PPX Events, or Island Kitchen to cater a private dinner. Both Lemon Press and Pip and Anchor do takeaway charcuterie boards. You'll want to stock up on wine, champagne, and spirits at either Nantucket Wine & Spirits or Hatch's.

There can be no proper bachelorette party without a trip to the Chicken Box or singing around the piano at the Club Car!

A fun "field trip" is climbing the steps to the top of the First Congregational Church tower.

ARE YOU COMING FOR A ROMANTIC GETAWAY?

I highly suggest, if your calendar allows, coming midweek just after Labor Day. Everything is still open but the crowds and families with children have gone back to school. The weather is still warm and the beaches are still hospitable for swimming.

I think it's most romantic to stay in town. Check out 76 Main Ink Press Hotel and stay in the "Elin" suite. Or splurge and see if there's a beachfront room at Cliffside Beach Club and spend your days lounging under an umbrella on Cliffside's private beach.

I suggest renting bikes from Nantucket Bike Shop or Young's Bicycle Shop, and if you're feeling hearty, ride out to Sconset, eat lunch in the Chanticleer garden, check out the Siasconset Union Chapel, walk across the drawbridge in town with the sundial, and wander the side streets admiring the tiny cottages. You can also enjoy the Sconset Bluff Walk all the way out to Sankaty Head Light. This is a lot of exercise, so place your bikes on the front of the Wave and catch a ride back to town.

The most romantic dinner venue in town is **Company of the Cauldron.** I didn't mention the Cauldron in the restaurant section because it's so specifically for couples. It's cozy and candlelit, and only one meal is served per night to everyone (with substitutions for vegetarians and people with allergies). So you'll want to check the menu to see if any of the week's offerings inspire. Chef Joseph Keller's food is nothing short of extraordinary.

If you're looking for a nightcap, I suggest the tucked-away bar at the **Ships Inn,** or join in with the singing at the Club Car.

ARE YOU ON A MOTHER-DAUGHTER TRIP?

Wonderful! Stay at the White Elephant Hotel and arrange to ride in the skiff up the harbor to Topper's at the Wauwinet for lunch on the deck. This is the height of elegance. After lunch, you can lounge on the lawn chairs as you digest your food before they bring you back. If you're up for shopping in town, don't miss Centre Pointe, Milly & Grace, the **Staud** pop-up, Nantucket Looms, and the bookstores. For a pick-me-up, grab a coffee or kombucha from Lemon Press. Then you may want to catch one of the productions at Theatre Workshop of Nantucket before going to your dinner at the Languedoc.

ARE YOU *JUST* A DAY-TRIPPER, TRYING TO SEE AS MUCH AS YOU CAN WITHOUT SPENDING THE NIGHT?

A mistake a lot of people make when they arrive by ferry is to eat and shop close to the ferry. I advise walking all the way to the top of Main Street, checking out the shops and the side streets as you go. (If you make it to Murray's Toggery Shop, you're in good shape.) On Wednesdays, you can join the line for my weekly signing at Mitchell's; this is a terrific place to make friends. For lunch, I have two fantastic suggestions. One is to walk to Jetties Beach and eat, feet in sand, at Sandbar. You can wander down this same road a little farther to check out Cliffside Beach Club, with its colorful umbrellas, and Galley Beach, which will likely be open for an Aperol spritz on the beach.

The other phenomenal lunch option, one that requires less walking, is to head back down toward the ferries and eat at Straight Wharf Fish Market, ideally at a table on the deck.

If time allows, make an afternoon visit to Bartlett's Ocean View Farm—the market and nursery are worth wandering through, especially in the fall—and then end your day with the quick walk from the farm to Cisco Brewers and get a late-afternoon snack or early dinner at one of the fine food trucks before heading back to the ferry.

HOW DO I LIVE LIKE A LOCAL?

Rent an Airbnb and a Jeep. Start your day early with coffee and a morning bun from Wicked Island Bakery. Then take a walk out in Sanford Farm, one of the trails maintained by the Nantucket Conservation Foundation. Be sure to bring water: this trail is not strenuous but it does stretch all the way to the south shore. After this adventure, you'll have worked up an appetite, so call in your sandwich order at Something Natural, get it from the pickup window, and head over to Steps Beach for a picnic and a swim. If the weather is nice, spend a lazy afternoon. If you're feeling froggy, head back into town to catch a movie at the Dreamland Theater. Dinner will be at the Seagrille, followed by an ice-cream cone at Island Kitchen. That's it. You're ready to move here.

Conclusion

Before I leave you, I'd like to say a few parting words about the island. I came to Nantucket in the summer of 1993 intending to stay for only the season and "write my book." (This was a novel called *Girl Stuff,* which never saw the light of day.) I was living in New York at the time, and when my summer on Nantucket ended and I returned to my apartment in Manhattan, I burst into tears. The person who had been subletting my apartment that summer (who happened to be my ex-boyfriend) looked at me and said, "I take it you had a good summer?" I knew then that my future would be on Nantucket; I moved to the island year-round the following June.

I had fallen in love with the island: the dunes and the eelgrass and the sandy roads that cut through the moors, the houses with names (!) and boot scrapers on the front steps and lavish flower boxes, the simple aesthetic of gray shingles with white trim, the days of fog and the days of bright sunshine, the singular pleasure of driving in a Jeep onto the beach and watching the sun set over the water at 40th Pole, the smell of butter and garlic as I walked into 21 Federal, the taste of corn picked from the fields of Bartlett's Farm only an hour before, the sensation every night of going to bed with sand in the sheets. But more than all of that, I fell in love with the people. It's the people of Nantucket who have made the island my home, and raising four children here has been a wonderful experience. The year-round community is diverse and vibrant. We are hearty folks, patient, tolerant, and there is no community that comes together to help one another like we do.

I owe Nantucket Island everything I have and everything I am. What a muse she has been—and what an utter delight it is to share her with you.

XO,
Elin

Credits

About the Author

Elin Hilderbrand is a graduate of the Johns Hopkins University and the University of Iowa Writers' Workshop. She is a cohost of the podcast *Books, Beach & Beyond* with @TimTalksBooks creator Tim Ehrenberg. Hilderbrand is raising four young adult children and likes to spend her free time at the beach and on her Peloton. She is a grateful eleven-year breast cancer survivor.

About the Illustrator

Artist Meredith Hanson crafts vibrant stories through her art, blending fine-art expertise with island inspiration. With a versatile background in oils, watercolors, acrylics, and pastels, she started her professional artistic journey on Nantucket, where she lived for twelve years. Now residing in Princeton, New Jersey, with her husband, Patrick, and their golden retriever, Willis, Hanson continues to paint and collaborate with Nantucket businesses, frequently returning to her beloved island for work and for summer retreats with her family.